Exile and Change in Renaissance Literature

Exile and Change in Renaissance Literature

A. BARTLETT GIAMATTI

YALE UNIVERSITY PRESS
NEW HAVEN AND LONDON

Published with the assistance of the
Elizabethan Club of Yale University from
the foundation established in memory
of Oliver Baty Cunningham of the Class of
1917, Yale College.

Designed by Sally Harris
and set in Garamond type by
The Saybrook Press, Inc.
Printed in the United States of America by
Vail-Ballou Press, Binghamton,
New York.

CHAPTER 1 is reprinted from *Play of
Double Senses: Spenser's Faerie Queene*,
A. Bartlett Giamatti
(Prentice-Hall, Inc., 1975).
CHAPTER 2 is reprinted from *Poetic
Traditions of the English Renaissance*, ed.
Maynard Mack and George DeForest
Lord (Yale University Press, 1982).
CHAPTER 3 is reprinted from *Italian
Literature: Roots and Branches*, ed.
Giose Rimanelli and Kenneth John
Atchity (Yale University Press, 1976).
CHAPTER 4 originally appeared in
Four Essays on Romance, ed.
Herschel Baker (Harvard University
Press, 1971), and is reprinted with
the permission of the publisher. © 1971
by the President and Fellows of
Harvard College.
CHAPTER 5 originally appeared in *First
Images of America: The Impact of the
New World on the Old*, ed. Fredi
Chiappelli et al. (University of
California Press, 1976), and is
reprinted with the permission of the
publisher. © 1976 by the Regents of
the University of California.
CHAPTER 6 is reprinted from
The Yale Review (Summer 1972).
CHAPTER 7 is reprinted from *The
Disciplines of Criticism*, ed. Peter
Demetz, Thomas Greene, and Lowry
Nelson, Jr. (Yale University Press,
1968).

Library of Congress Cataloging in Publication Data

Giamatti, A. Bartlett.
  Exile and change in Renaissance literature.

  Includes bibliographical references and index.
  1. European literature—Renaissance, 1450—1600—
History and criticism—Addresses, essays, lectures.
I. Title.
PN721.G52   1984   820'.9'003   83-12561
ISBN 0-300-03074-6

10 9 8 7 6 5 4 3 2 1

For
T. S. G.
and
Marcus, Elena, and Paul

Contents

Preface

The essays included in this collection all had their origin in a larger project, first mapped out some fifteen years ago. I had in mind then a major study of the impact of the Italian Renaissance on the English Renaissance, focusing on relationships between those two cultures as defined by literary forms and written documents.

It was clear to me from the outset that many would be the exploratory forays before such a journey could be begun in earnest, and these essays (written for various occasions, including a small book on Spenser) are those forays. I had conceived of the project as a study in translation, concerned with the carrying over to another shore of a cultural and literary vision, in all its variety. I was interested to explore what was lost and what was gained in such a multifaceted act of translation, and I hoped to engage the problem that writers in Italy and England (and to some extent in France and Spain) confronted in bringing ancient ethics, literature, and learning to life again between the fourteenth and seventeenth centuries.

Of that larger plan, suggestive of the issues we embrace in thinking of cultural renewal, these fragments remain, and I hope they may be of use to students and scholars. I believe these essays are linked by more than simply their common origin in a larger design. Many of them return to the question of origins themselves, both in their overt preoccupations and in their style of composition. I look often for the origin of a given topic or mythological obsession and also probe the various writers' own return to the question of beginnings.

More specifically, two themes recur, those of change and of exile. In the search for beginnings from a position in the middle, Renaissance writers are constantly struck by and fearful of the inevitable change that gives them life and corrodes their spirit. Mutability is Spenser's word, but it is his age's preoccupation. The long essay on Proteus, the first foray I made, examines the ubiquity of the concern with metamorphosis and strives to find a methodology responsive to Renaissance culture's own preoccupation with a figure from Greek mythology. The other theme running through much of what is here is the sense of exile, of being peripheral or distant from the ancients, and is the matter of the essay on Hippolytus, the last to be written. The Renaissance's constant quest to create an authentic identity was always hindered by the sense of being a mere reproduction of the ancient culture upon which one wished to pattern one's literature and life.

The Renaissance is an act, as Boccaccio says in another context, of "rescribere," of rewriting, of writing down again, every time different from the last time, no time sufficient to create what was lost, each act of recreation a counterfeit original. Our condition, whether as individuals or as a culture, is to be exiled, and that exile in all its changes is now all there is.

In the years since these essays were written, I have turned to other duties and other kinds of writing. I do not claim a grand design for what has occurred since I ceased to live among the authors approached in these essays; I can say that their radical concern with making a civil culture, where ethical and aesthetic values cohere with integrity, has also continued to be mine, as has the Renaissance's unshakable belief in humanistic education, the leading out of private learning toward the good of the larger public. Rhetorically based, philological in method, and inclusive of values in perspective, the program for education that was Humanism did not deny the religious traditions of the Christian West in favor of the ethics of antiquity. It rather sought to reconcile all the traditions that teachers, thinkers, civil servants, rulers, and poets then embraced. Our modern sensibility began with those who grappled with multiplicity in knowledge, in information, in technology, in values, in perspectives on time and space, in worlds beyond the seas and in the heavens, in forms of freedom and in needs for constraint. To reduce Humanism to teaching a grammatical system or to research in texts or to a political view of civic virtue or, as current parlance has it, to a secular denial of the claims of the spirit is to reduce it to something neat, and false. The very intellectual or ideological act of reduction is itself false to the diversity of motive and manifestation that Humanism displayed.

I have attempted to correct misprints and errors in these essays. I have not brought up to date the bibliographic portions. My debts to other scholars are noted throughout. Here I wish to thank again all the students, undergraduate and graduate, who listened patiently and who taught me over the years. I also thank the John Simon Guggenheim Foundation, which awarded me a fellowship for 1969–70 during which I began work on the original project on Italy and England. I note particularly the assistance of Stephen B. Cushman and Shane S. Gasbarra, who have helped prepare various of the essays and indeed the whole volume for the printer. Their assistance has been expert and invaluable, and I am in their debt. Neither they nor anyone else bears any responsibility for the errors and lapses that remain. Finally, I thank the two readers for the Yale University Press, whose comments were most helpful and encouraging. I also thank my copyeditor, Mary Alice Galligan, for her skill, and particularly my editor, Ellen Graham, for her unfailing editorial wisdom and her patience.

A. BARTLETT GIAMATTI

April 4, 1983
New Haven, Connecticut

1

The Forms of Epic

Names, deeds, grey legends, dire events, rebellions,
Majesties, sovran voices, agonies,
Creations and destroyings, all at once
Pour into the wide hollow of my brain.
Keats, *Hyperion*, III. 114–17

In the third book of the *Aeneid*, Aeneas tells Dido and her court of the
Trojan disaster and how finally he and his men reached Buthrotum, a
Greek city ruled by Priam's son Helenus and his consort, Andromache, Hector's widow. In Aeneas' account, we learn a fundamental
lesson of the poem: One must rid oneself of the past in order to build
the future. Buthrotum was meant to be a replica of Troy in every
detail, but the brook intended to duplicate the Simois is dry and the
tomb of Hector where Andromache worships and weeps is empty.
Everywhere we see the sadness and futility, the melancholy sterility,
of living in and living off the past. With Aeneas, we learn to look
forward, not back; forward to the new city, the new hope—not
another Troy, not even a new Carthage, but Rome. With the hero,
we fix on that high walled place where, as Anchises tells his son
in the depths of Book VI, the fine arts will be "to rule nations,
to crown peace with law / And to spare the conquered and to
conquer the proud" (VI. 851–53). "Sic pater Anchises." So said the
father.

I

So said the father, who is a central figure in epic, whether he is called Jove or Priam or Anchises or Charlemagne or God. So the father, who gives us life, teaches us to live together. And in revealing this civilizing impulse through the father, these large, public, historically oriented poems unfold their massive subject: man's effort to impose civilization within and without himself, his desire and need to earn citizenship in a city of man or of God. So the father tells the son in the underworld, that deep, dark place in the self where the roots of the self begin, and so the son learns to be a father, to his people, to his city, to himself.

This view forward, however, that reveals the glories of the civilized life and that justifies the process whereby fathers make fathers of their sons, is not the only view epic offers. There is also the view back, toward the ruined city of Troy that, like Priam, slipped in its own blood. This is the view not of what we should or must be but of what we have been and are. If epics justify the ways of fathers to sons, they also reveal the ways of sons to fathers, the explosive, anarchic ways in which new growth means forcible tearing and sundering from the old. This view back sees how death, decay, and desolation underlie all our best hopes. And so one notices in epic poems the constant sense that what we create and build—selves, families, cities—will always be prey to time and change, for what can escape? What city, what Troy or Athens, Rome or London, can last? Every epic poet who knows how glorious Troy was also knows that its fate will come to us all.

One can say the epic is a profoundly political kind of poem, if we take *political* as it is derived from the Greek *polis*, city, and thus is concerned with the way men live in community. But we mistake this political preoccupation if we regard epic only as celebrating creation and hymning the order and goodly government of things. Epic does sing of order, but out of necessity as much as delight; for epic is profoundly aware of the forces that destroy, of the disease and savage loneliness within man that renders so much of his human effort futile. The *Iliad*, after all, ends with the imminent destruction of a city; the festive *Odyssey* culminates with a vast feast hall littered with dead bodies. And the *Aeneid* begins with Troy in flames and ends with another city conquered, as, in the name of fatherhood and civilization, Aeneas becomes another Achilles, and brutal Turnus another Hector, killed before a conquered town. *Paradise Lost*, for all the hopes and promises of redemption, ends with the solitary pair wandering past flaming swords, exiled from the garden that was a perfect earthly image of God's city. The great civilizing passage of the son to fatherhood, of the individual to an institution, cannot be accomplished without pain and loss. "For nothing can be sole or whole," says Yeats, "that has not been rent."

In many ways, great epics illuminate man's need and man's incapacity to control the demonic and destructive forces within him and around him. Great epics all celebrate what man can make, and the poem itself is the chief image of that power. But these very poems also tell of the futility of man's efforts to subdue and contain the same potent forces he has tapped. We will return more than once to that mystery at the heart of epic, to that mix or mingle of the creative and destructive, of growth and decay, of order and monstrosity. We will examine often the way epic probes that basic human dilemma, whereby love and hate are fed by the same nerve, whereby the forces of life are also the agents of death. We cannot escape the epic's focus on the way we obey the law of fatherhood while denying what is best in the father we love.

I

"Quidve sequens tantos possim superare labores?" (*Aeneid* III. 368) So Aeneas at Buthrotum asked his host Helenus, who is a seer: "By what course can I overcome such suffering?" *Labores*, the Virgilian *labor*, effort, work, the expenditure of energy: Here the great word (and virtue) carries a note of travail and weariness. Aeneas is asking: How can I get home? What must I do? What will it cost me in terms of myself? What is it going to take to establish stability? These are the questions epics always ask. But the basic question in epic, because these poems always "know" where they are going, is: How do we get there? Thus the old idea of epic as a quest, a seeking in the world—to destroy Troy or to found Rome, to defeat the Infidel for King and Cross, find the Grail, free Jerusalem, see the face of God, discover India or Peru, worship at the court of the glorious Faery Queene. The idea of the quest is a basic and useful one. From another perspective, however, epics are equally about exile, for the quest is often to get home, to get back to those roots where one lives at harmony with oneself. The quest is the search for where we began, the end of our exile from what we love: in the *Odyssey*, our exile from Ithaca and Penelope; in the *Iliad*, the exile from Helen, for that is why they go to Troy; our exile from Beatrice and God, in Dante's *Comedy*; our exile from Elizabeth and her court, in Spenser's *Faerie Queene*.

The epic is often concerned with exile and the way back, and woman is always at the center. She is often both the goal and the obstacle. She is Penelope who waits and Circe who delays. She is Dido, who slows us, and Rome—Roma, the feminine place—who calls us on. Sometimes she is both the reason we wander and the object we seek, because only where she is are we at home. Such a woman is Helen, or Eve, Eve who causes our exile from the Garden and from the Father, and Eve with whom we find a new homestead and by whose sons we become fathers ourselves. Always obeying the law of paternity, defying the father who loves us.

We come back to the center of epic, that core of experience where our humanity is defined by the contradictions it encompasses. We return to that heart of the epic where our urge to be reconciled in harmony is the same urge that tears us into solitary fragments. But whether we see epic as emphasizing quest or exile, the impulse to go out and make cities, or to go home and rest; whether we stress the contradictory nature of fatherhood, or womanhood—in short, whether we opt for the specific focus of the *Iliad* or that of the *Odyssey* (and finally they are always mixed), we are taught that all human enterprise and endeavor involve a long, weary way. That to get *there* means going a long, long distance, a long space in time. We cannot escape epic's long view: that rest will come by never resting, that peace will come only by war, that all your future will be devoted, despite yourself and at best, to finding a memory from the past.

And so Helenus, inspired by Apollo, tells Aeneas how he must go, where to stop, what to avoid. When you see Scylla and Charybdis, he says, Scylla a maiden above, a monster below—again, the inexplicable, double image of woman in the midst of the journey—when you see her, better double back, and, lingering, fetch a double compass, "circumflectere cursus." Better, in short, go the long way around. And this long way around is precisely the way he goes and is the way all epic moves, as the poem itself charts for the reader the course that the poem describes. The epic poem, oblique, indirect, always digressive, interpolating tales, pausing for breath—the poet's, the hero's, ours—is itself always moving toward its own goal, its own completed fixity and revealed pattern. Yet while the poem is going home, so to speak, it seems as aimless as we are in our lives. It seems always to choose the long way around, which is finally the only way, as every poet and every man knows for himself.

He "winds with ease / Through the pure marble Air his oblique way," and later:

> With tract oblique
> At first, as one who sought access but feared
> To interrupt, side-long he works his way.

So in *Paradise Lost* Milton describes Satan, as escaped fiend in Book III, as subtle snake in Book IX. But Milton also describes the way his poem works, the way he works as a poet, and the way all epics and their poets work.

Often we grow impatient with epic poems. Too long, we feel—all those irrelevant interruptions, those additions, conventions, invocations, interpolations, those stories and speeches, catalog and dull history. But these are all part of the journey, the reader's journey on his long way around. For just as there are epic poets, involved in the task of creating, and just as there are epic heroes, who labor to create, so also are there epic readers. And all those digressions and history and stretches of catalog, all those elements of the poem which image the vastness and variety of the real world, allow the epic poet to involve the epic reader in the meaning of the poem, which is the immense difficulty of getting *there* and the driving necessity to go.

The great length of the epic, the vast meandering, is meant to communicate the laborious and perhaps futile effort of the hero and poet to master all the stuff of history and experience. For whether one is an epic protagonist caught in the massive world of contingency, or the epic poet trying to bring order from the chaos of mankind's memories, or the epic reader trying to get through the long poem, in each case one is attempting to limit the seemingly limitless, striving to control and master the seemingly endless. The reader's confrontation with the huge poem imitates the epic hero's confrontation with his vast world, and in both cases man's need for control and his need for completion are stretched to their utmost.

The long way around or digressive techniques of epic also serve another purpose. By lingering or pausing or turning back, the epic poet includes an immense amount in order to image the apparently endless complexity we humans must face. But the poet also proceeds obliquely so he will have enough room for his historical concerns. The epic poet's problem is that he must have enough space for all of time. His historical concerns come in many forms, but whatever they are, secular or divine, national, social, or individual, or all of these at once, the poet often focuses on another kind of history as well. He often focuses on literary history; for, particularly by the Renaissance, literary history is a fundamental concern and basic tool of the poet. In the Renaissance, epic is not only the queen of the genres; it is also the most literary genre.

Epic poets are immensely concerned with other epic poems; that is, a given poet is constantly and overtly looking over his shoulder at his predecessors' poems. For instance, in a letter to Spenser, Gabriel Harvey says he thinks Spenser's (now lost) *Nine Comedies* no more approach Ariosto's than "that *Eluish Queene* doth to his *Orlando Furioso*, which notwithstanding, you wil needes seeme to emulate, and hope to overgo, as you flatly professed yourself in one of your last letters" (Grosart, *Works*, I.95). If Spenser, in a letter now lost, did flatly profess his desire to emulate and to "overgo" the *Orlando Furioso* with his *Faerie Queene*, then he was simply responding to his great predecessor in the habitual fashion of epic poets. Ariosto had hoped to overgo Boiardo, whose unfinished poem Ariosto took up and continued; Boiardo, as he makes clear, intended to unify and thus supersede all the *chansons de geste* about Charlemagne, on the one hand, and the Arthurian romances that he had inherited from the Middle Ages, on the other. Of course, Virgil is the model, for the Renaissance clearly recognized that the first six books of the *Aeneid* are an *Odyssey*, the second six an *Iliad*. It is the deepest desire of the epic poet to overgo his forerunners in the art; we see this best with Milton, who surpassed them all.

At *Paradise Lost*, I.16, Milton announces the aim of his "adventurous Song" to pursue "Things unattempted yet in Prose or Rhyme." When we hear this grand vaunt, we are thrilled. And we are no less thrilled when we realize that Ariosto begins the *Orlando Furioso* with precisely the same words (I.ii) and that Boiardo begins the *Orlando Innamorato* substantially the same way (I.i.1)—all in imitation of Horace in the first ode of Book III. Nor is our pleasure in Milton's boast diminished when we find that Spenser, *Faerie Queene*, VI.proem.2, and Dante, *Divine Comedy, Paradise*, II.6, also said the same thing. Nothing is more traditional than the claim to be making an innovation.

The point is that we are expected to know the claim has been made before. From the poet's point of view, we *must* know of the boast's previous existence, else we will not recognize the significance of the most recent poet's achievement. Epic poems, ever since antiquity the noblest form of poetry, for which the high style was reserved, must contain and include all that went before; and that means all previous encyclopedic efforts at inclusion, all previous epic poems. Thus Renaissance poets ennoble their matter by consciously surpassing previous literary images of nobility. One sense in which epics are literarily self-conscious is their view of themselves as inheritors and containers of previous epic literature.

The reason the epic seeks to store previous literature emerges when we consider the epic poet's immense task: to sum up a vision of the society or history or condition of man at his largest and best. With all human history at stake, through individuals or through a nation, the task of including man's creations and aspirations and failures becomes more difficult the more there is. However, if epics in particular or literature in general distill the essence of a time or belief, of a culture or society, then by referring to literature, we can make reference to life. If we believe the *Aeneid* contains those values Rome esteemed most, then we can refer to those values—patriotic, religious, communal, legal—by taking the long way around and implicating, involving, borrowing from, echoing, and alluding to the *Aeneid*. Thus literary history can be made an analogue to human history. To refer within your epic to other epics is to create and sustain a shorthand by which you refer to all that came before. By this shorthand, the poet proves that his patron or nation or language, his values and culture, his poem, is superior because it knows, and can include, all that came before, all there is to know. To satisfy their encyclopedic thrust, epic poems include and exploit previous literature as the only way of storing previous life.

In its quest for completeness, the epic stores within itself all kinds of literature. What A.S.P. Woodhouse has said of *The Faerie Queene* can be said of most great epic poems of the Renaissance:

> There is scarcely a genre that it does not involve or draw on—epic narrative, chivalric quest, the whole range of allegorical poetry . . . not to mention pastoral, emblem, idyll, interlude and masque.[1]

The list might even be extended, but Mr. Woodhouse's point is well made. Epic inclusiveness is just that—the urge to know and absorb all forms of experience. Thus, to include forms of experience, epic includes literary forms; to contain all kinds of life, it contains all the kinds of literature. Each of these literary kinds, or genres, has a different type of psychic appeal; each literary kind summons and involves a different level of the mind, a different set of reactions, a different pattern of feeling. Each brings to bear on human activity a different perspective. And all these different ways of seeing, in their cunning juxtaposition and arrangement, bring new insight, new versions of vision.

Thus the epic reader is forced to correct his sight, adjust his gaze, and absorb new or renewed experience, for the very act of reading the epic poem, with its multiple versions of human reality, its various literary kinds, is itself a new experience. Epic becomes what it describes: It embodies the varieties of literature in order to display life's various modes. Epic literature, either as the various genres in careful array or as the whole called epic narrative, is thus constantly urging us to take it seriously as a way of stretching and radically reforming the mind.

II

My emphasis on the literary self-consciousness of Renaissance epic may create the impression that Renaissance poets were mistaking art for life and were substituting the appearance of things as created by art for the reality of life as created by God. Did the Renaissance poet in fact think he was God? No, but he saw himself like God—Spenser says a "godlike man" (IV.ii.1)—omniscient, omnipotent, the creator of plenitude and variety, a maker (that old word for poet) of a micro-cosmos. However, no Renaissance poet ever proposed that fiction is reality. Indeed, the final sense in which we can speak of the Renaissance epic's literary self-consciousness is the sense poets had of their epics' status as *poems*, as artifacts, as things—to adapt Tasso's words—"made," not "born" (*Gerusalemme Liberata*, XIV.48). Renaissance poets knew better than anyone that their powers were only God-like, and not God's. They well knew that their poems were only images of reality, not the thing itself. And like other forms of knowledge, they included this knowledge in their poems. Renaissance epics become virtually obsessed with the problems of art and nature, illusion and reality; they constantly examine the deceitfulness of appearances, and return again and again to the creation of fictions, myths, conventions, codes, constructs, artifacts.

Epic poems of the Renaissance are concerned with the imposition of order to create new versions of life; that is, they are in a sense concerned with poetry. But these epics are themselves such versions of experience, such illusions of reality—and if one of the lessons they teach is that words, fictions, appearances are misleading or dangerous, then how can we trust the very poem that conveys this message? The poems become instances of the problem they propose to examine. They are creations in language that warn against the power of words. In short, Renaissance epics often teach us not to trust Renaissance epics. They force us back toward life, civic and active; they urge us to learn, by reading, how to live—not how to substitute books for the world.

We see this thrust everywhere: in Ariosto's concern to show how the codes and conventions of chivalry are fictions we create to gull ourselves into believing the world is working the way we want it to; in Spenser's constant warnings against taking what appears for what is; above all, in Cervantes' great book *Don Quixote*, whose fundamental preoccupation is books. After all the emphasis in poetry on the fallibility and instability of language, Cervantes' great swan song of chivalric romance in the Renaissance takes as its subject a man who mistakes poems for life, literary epics for real experience. Cervantes' book carries the epic's literary self-consciousness to its logical conclusion and, among other things, is about the power of illusion and language to destroy. *Don Quixote* virtually begins with a scene in which many of the books upon which *Don Quixote* is based are burned (I.vi). As the housekeeper, niece, barber, and priest preside over the Inquisition and consign the offending books to the flames in the courtyard below, we have the most graphic image in Renaissance literature for the destructive impulses in Renaissance literature. Here the seeds in epic that contained the destruction of epic are allowed to flower, paradoxically in a book most memorable for the elements it sought to extinguish.

So, the twin impulses of epic: to show man imposing order, while conveying the futility of trying to control chaos; to show the foundation of cities, while taking us across space and time littered with decayed cities and with human landscapes where the "mansion of mortality," the "castle of health," as Spenser says, is dying and diseased. As the epic proposes limitless horizons against which man must raise limits, and implies that the effort may be for nought, so the epic before Milton (for *Paradise Lost* is the exception in many ways) is a creation aware always of its own fallibility. It is an illusion warning against appearances; it is made of words ever whispering, precisely amidst the glories and virtues they conjure, not to trust conjurers—not to trust anything save God, who is unavailable save by faith.

The epic poet of the Renaissance, who had to know everything, knew too much. He knew, as Spenser knew and says in so many ways, that art can bind up the wounds of time; words can freeze change into something eternal; poems can move out of time, for all time. But he also knew art was not life, or true pleasure, or real virtue, but only a painted scene, and that to mistake what seems for what is would be to commit the error his poem warns against. Since the Fall there is no perfection save in art, and that is superb but not, finally, true.

2

Hippolytus among the Exiles:
The Romance of Early Humanism

Exile was a central and abiding preoccupation of Petrarch's life, as it would be for that cultural epoch, the Renaissance, that he seems to initiate. In his fragmentary autobiographical piece, the *Letter to Posterity*, written near the end of his life, Petrarch says:

> Honestibus parentibus, Florentinis origine, fortuna mediocri et (ut verum fatear) ad inopiam vergente, sed patria pulsis, Aretti in exilio natus sum, anno huius aetatis ultimae, quae a Christo incipit, M. CCC. IIII. die Lunae, ad auroram XIII. Cal. Augusti.

> My parents were worthy people, of Florentine origin, middling well-off, indeed, to confess the truth, on the edge of poverty. As they were expelled from their home city, I was born in exile in Arezzo, in the 1304th year of Christ's era, at dawn on a Monday, the 20th of July. [1]

Or again, in the prefatory epistle to his *Familiares*, or *Letters on Familiar Affairs* (that massive epic of the self in twenty-four books, comprising 350 letters written between 1325 and 1366), Petrarch tells his closest friend, the Belgian musician Lodewyck Heyliger, whom he called "Socrates":

> Ulysseos errores erroribus meis confer: profecto si nominis et rerum claritas una foret, nec diutius erravit ille, nec latius. Ille patrios fines iam senior excessit: cum nihil in ulla aetate longum sit, omnia sunt in senectute brevissima. Ego in exilio genitus, in exilio natus sum.

Compare my wanderings with those of Ulysses; if we were equal in name and fame, it would be known that he traveled no longer or farther than I. He was a mature man when he left his hometown; though nothing lasts long at any age, everything runs very fast in old age. But I was conceived in exile and born in exile.[2]

"Ego in exilio genitus, in exilio natus sum." "Ego . . . sum"—his deepest concern: "genitus," "natus"—the life of man: and through it, balancing and ordering the terse, pregnant span of the sentence, and the life, the dominant chord—"in exilio," "in exilio." This is January 1350.

Petrarch's whole existence, his sense of himself, would be determined by his obsession with origin and exile; by his conviction that he was displaced and marginal. Unlike Ulysses, who wandered but came home, he, Petrarch, was never at home save in books. Only in books, and in words, did he feel at peace and at rest, only then not moving, as he says in the broken last sentence of his *Letter to Posterity*, "like a sick man, to be rid of distress by shifting position" ("studio more egrorum loci mutatione tediis consulendi").[3] Petrarch's odyssey, his endless exile, depended—as his courtship of Laura depended—on not achieving what he said he desired. His sense of identity depended on being displaced, for only in perpetual exile could Petrarch gain the necessary perspective on himself truly to determine, or create, who he was. Only by being eccentric, could he center, or gather in and collect, his self.[4] Exile was essential to his view of himself, and it was, as we will see, essential in varying ways to his culture's view of itself. Both Petrarch, the individual, and humanism, the dominant elite culture of Europe for the next three centuries, had to assert exile, whether from secular antiquity and its ethics or scriptural Paradise and its bliss, in order to refashion, or revive, or give rebirth to, or regain, what had once been purer, holier, or simply more whole.

For the Renaissance, integration of self and culture meant seeing Origin or the Original as distant and lost, so that one could imitate and emulate and thus make oneself a new copy or assert a genuine revision. A seminal tension in Renaissance culture, as in individuals like Petrarch, stems from the conviction that, on the one hand, origins so distant were also for the first time clearly perceived after the darkness, but that, on the other hand, what was recreated on that clear model would never be truly authentic. The Renaissance, for all its assertive, expansive, cultural imperialism—its revival of the past, its new texts, institutions and perceptions—would never completely shake the sense that what it made was removed, not quite worthy of the original; if not second-rate, at least secondhand, just as beneath the oft-repeated boast of each people that their land had been colonized by a hero from Troy—Italy by Aeneas, France by Francus, Portugal by the sons of Lusus, Britain by Brutus—there would be the constant awareness that Europe was founded by the losers, that the European people were colonists who, for all their glory, were exiled from the homeland, that in the Westering of culture, much had been gained but something had also been lost.

But this is to anticipate the sixteenth century, the end of the Renaissance, and we are at the beginning, in the fourteenth, and my point is simple: exile is the precondition to identity.[5] So Petrarch, never truly at home, always refuses to return. In March 1351, Giovanni Boccaccio carries to Padua a letter to Petrarch from the governors of Florence promising restitution of his patrimony and a chair at their new university. Petrarch writes two letters of refusal—one, to Zanobi da Strada (*Ep. Met.* III.8) in early 1351, saying he must bear his exile with equanimity; the other, to the Priors and People of Florence (*Fam.*, XI.5) of April 1351, thanking them but saying the Pope had called him to Avignon. He needed his exile. And we get even better insight into why he needed it in two letters (*Fam.* II.3−4) to an otherwise unknown correspondent, Severo Appennini-cola, letters of consolation for the other's fate. Since the letters are long, I shall summarize.

The letter to Appenninicola begins with an etymology of "exilium," a derivation not remarkable in itself but interesting because the etymologizing habit, the philological cast of mind, is, of course, typical of the whole humanist effort to uncover and reconstitute meaning by returning to origins. Whether through single words or whole bodies of texts, philology reaffirms the humanist's exile from true meaning as he struggles to overcome it. We shall return to this philological impulse. Then Petrarch goes on to say that exile resides in one's attitude when one is outside one's homeland; if one feels beaten, one is an exile; if one goes with dignity, one is a traveler. Exile consists of an attitude; the attitude is the fear of loss—loss of riches, fame, life. Exile is therefore an error in judgment, and anyone can make this error. But, and Petrarch adopts the perspective of his correspondent:

> Quod si tu mihi, quicumque a patria absunt exulare sine ulla distinctione firmaveris, rari ergo non exules. Quis enim hominum, nisi desidiosus ac mollis, non aliquotiens aut visendi avidus, aut discendi studio, aut illustrandi animi, aut curandi corporis, aut amplificandae rei familiaris proposito, aut necessitate bellorum, aut suae reipublicae seu domini seu parentis imperio, domum linquit et patriam?

> If you firmly believe that whoever is absent from his native land is without question an exile, where are those who are not exiles? For what man, unless he were lazy and soft, has not departed from his home and his native land several times either because he was desirous of seeing new things, or of learning, or of enlightening his mind, or was concerned about his health, or was desirous of increasing his wealth, or because of the demands of wars, or at the command of his state, of his master, of his parents?[6]

But Petrarch explains—and this is the heart of the matter—one can be forced into exile, but not forced to despair of returning:

> Vidimus in exilium missos, priusquam ad destinatum pervenissent, immenso patriae desiderio revocatus: alios vero, post tempus, tanto cum honore . . . reversos. . . . Nemo unquam tam iniquo loco iacuit, ut non ei liceret oculos attollere: nemo tam deploratum rerum suarum vidit exitum, ut prohibetur sperare meliora.

> We have seen men sent into exile who, before they had arrived at their destination, were called back to the homeland because of the unbearable grief of the citizens. Others, after a long time, returned with so much honor. . . . No one was committed to such a horrible place that

he was not allowed to raise his eyes; no one viewed the loss of his belongings as so deplorable that he was unable to hope for better things.[7]

Let us pause here, for it strikes me that there is more at issue than simply a moralizing injunction to be optimistic. Petrarch, in his meditation on exile, is saying not that one will, or even should, come home, but that the hope of returning is ever alive—indeed, that the hope of returning home is as strong as the force that sends one away in the first place. The man who would not go home always had to believe he could. Indeed, much as life—for Petrarch—was an endless marginality, so also was it sustained, precisely because of that marginality, by the belief that one might become central. Petrarch's need to believe he was displaced was the only way he could believe in genuine return, revival, recall.

This perspective is what we may call "the romance of early humanism"—the secondary culture's deep belief that, despite distance and loss, it might become primary; the conviction that, through effort and emulation, the copy might become an original, the removed might restore the beginning, the exile might—through purposeful wandering—become a point, or recapture the point, of origin. Petrarch tells his friend to imitate the virtue of those ancients in exile, so that he may not despair that what has been done so often cannot be done again. And as he goes on, he seems to be saying: as we imitate the virtue of the ancients, we become virtuous; as we become virtuous, we are at home; we are at home because we are at one with the ancients, and they are our home. So he writes in 1359 to his beloved Socrates: "Homeland is for a man in any niche in the universe; only by impatience can he make himself believe [he is] in exile" ("Patriam viro omnem mundi angulum, exilium nusquam esse, nisi quod impatientia fecerit").[8]

He is groping for a definition; to call this a "theory" of exile is to make it sound too systematic, too abstract. He is working out, constantly, his attitudes toward exile, always fixing his intuitions in the balanced periods of his prose, his style both affirming his distance from the ancients and seeking, by imitation, to bridge that gulf. For it was finally the ancients, not Florence, or friends, or Tuscany, that Petrarch felt most exiled from, and because he expressed this perspective so powerfully, Renaissance culture, after him, would imitate him—both in his sense of exile and his efforts to return.

Petrarch's radical solitude stemmed from what we would call his sense of history. "He would have liked," says Peter Burke, "to have lived in Augustan Rome. For him, the period before the conversion of Constantine (the *aetas antiqua*) was an age of light; the *aetas nova*, the modern age which succeeded it, was an age of darkness. This was the reversal of the traditional Christian distinction."[9] Others, like Flavio Biondo, after him would speak of a "media aetas" between antiquity and the present; and still later others, like Vasari, would speak of the present as a "rebirth."[10] But the essential perspective on the ancients as distinct, distant, and the home we had left was established by Petrarch and his language of exile.

His efforts to find his true self in their selves is expressed in everything he wrote but never more clearly, or poignantly, than in the last ten letters of the last book, the twenty-fourth, of his *Familiares*—written between 1345 and 1360 to the great figures of antiquity. These letters, two to Cicero, one each to Seneca, Varro, Quintilian, Livy, Pollio, and then, building to the summit of poets and receding in time, to Horace, Virgil and Homer, are meditations on his distance from them, his desire to be with them. They are exercises in exile: fruitless efforts to go home that at the same time allow Petrarch to create himself. We need only look at one of these letters, keeping in mind what exile means for Petrarch, to see where the course of Renaissance humanism would run for some time to come. This is the fifth letter in the series, to Quintilian.

Petrarch wrote to Quintilian on 7 December 1350, the very day when, passing through Florence on his way to Rome, he was given an incomplete manuscript of Quintilian's *Institutes* by a young scholar named Lapo di Castiglionchio. Deeply moved, Petrarch wrote a lovely letter, finally praising Quintilian himself for being a great man, but saying, "greater than you, your highest merit lay in your ability to ground and to mold great men" ("magnus fateor vir fuisti,

sed instituendis formandisque magnis viris maximus"). [11] Shape others as he may, however, it is Quintilian's own shape that concerns
Petrarch most and that draws his attention in the opening lines:
"Your book, called *Institutes of Oratory*, has come to my hands, but
alas how mangled and mutilated. I recognize therein the hand of
time—the destroyer of all things" ("Oratoriarum institutionum liber
heu! discerptus et lacer venit ad manus meas. Agnovi aetatem vasta-
tricem omnium"). [12] Then, after saying how he admires Quintilian,
Petrarch returns to his figure again: "I saw the dismembered limbs of
a beautiful body and admiration mingled with grief seized me"
("Vidi formosi corporis artus effusos: admiratio animum dolorque
concussit"). [13]

This language for the incomplete book is crucial for what humanism would come to mean: the text is a beautiful body, a "corpus"
whose limbs are scattered, a body mutilated and mangled. Petrarch
uses the words *discerptus*, from *discerpere* ("to mutilate") and *lacer*,
meaning mangled, lacerated. The words have their own enormous
resonances. *Discerptus* for instance, is the word Virgil uses in the
Fourth Georgic (l. 522) to describe the mutilated Orpheus; *lacer* occurs
in *Aeneid* VI.495 to describe how Deiphobus appeared to Aeneas in
the underworld; and it is used again in *Aeneid* IX.491 to describe
Euryalus, he who fell as a purple flower cut by the plow. Potent
words, and images, for anyone steeped—as Petrarch was—in Virgil.
But I would suggest that beneath the image of the book as mutilated
body, beneath Deiphobus and Euryalus and even Orpheus, another
Virgilian passage is buried so deep that Petrarch does not seem to
know it, though others, imitating him, would almost instinctively
bring it to the surface. This is *Aeneid* VII.765–73, describing the
death of Hippolytus and his resurrection at the hands of Aesculapius:

> namque ferunt fama Hyppolytum, postquam arte novercae
> occiderit patriasque explerit sanguine poenas
> turbatis distractus equis, ad sidera rursus
> aetheria et superas caeli venisse sub auras,
> Paeoniis revocatum herbis et amore Dianae.
> tum pater omnipotens, aliquem indignatus ab umbris

mortalem infernis ad lumina surgere vitae,
ipse repertorem medicinae talis et artis
fulmine Phoebigenam Stygias detrusit ad undas.

For they tell how that Hippolytus, when he fell by a Stepmother's
    craft,
and slaked his father's vengeance in blood,
ripped apart by terrified horses, came again to the starry firmament,
and heaven's upper air, recalled by the Healer's
herbs and the love of Diana. Then the Father
omnipotent, angry that any mortal should rise
from the nether shades to the light of life,
hurled with his thunder beneath the Stygian waves
the finder of such healing-craft, him Apollo-born.[14]

Virgil goes on to say that Hippolytus, now named Virbius, was
taken to live out his life in Italy, and that his son, also Virbius, now
rode another chariot to join the army of Turnus.[15] I suggest this
passage, in conjunction with Petrarch's images of Quintilian mutilated, for two reasons. Here again, as with Deiphobus, Euryalus, and
Orpheus, we are dealing with the story of a lacerated body, and this
time with the story of one who came back, one who was "revocatus,"
says Virgil, as Petrarch's exiled ancients were sometimes recalled, "to
the starry firmament and heaven's upper air." Jove was angry that one
should go from "the nether shades to the light of life," but Hippolytus did it—then to find a home in Italy. His healer was punished
with exile to Hell, but the shredded Hippolytus came home again,
whole.

I suggest that in the story of Hippolytus and Aesculapius we have a
version of what I have been calling the romance of early humanism—
the sense that return or rebirth or restoration of origin and original
form is possible, a hope that not only sustained but necessitated
Petrarch's sense of exile. I suggest that in the mutilated body of
Hippolytus, mangled like those other Virgilian heroes but older than
all save Orpheus, Petrarch might see a figure for the shapes of all those
ancients, now known only in fragmentary texts, in mangled corpora,
whom he desired to see whole, and be with—if not one of. And I

suggest, lest you think I lack the courage of my aberrations, that in Aesculapius, the healer who could not be cured, the victim of his own powers, the scion of Apollo to whom the light was denied, Petrarch might see figured the humanist's power to restore—texts, bodies, traditions—and also his inability to experience the integrity, the wholeness, thus wrought.[16] A humanist might see the endless dialectic of his own dilemma—always being exiled so that he might find himself, always bringing the curative balm of ancient ethics to his culture, yet himself shifting like a sick man in distress.

II

I cannot prove that the Virgilian story of Hippolytus and Aesculapius is the link that binds Petrarch's sense of his and his culture's exile to his desire to integrate himself by restoring the fragments of the past; but I do know that humanists would use a language alluding to exile, fragmented bodies, and Aesculapius shortly after Petrarch, in ways that would have been impossible, I think, without him. And I know it is possible once again to affirm that if Petrarch did not create all the formulations humanism would use for itself, he did at least define the fundamental issues to which those formulations would respond—and those were the issues of how one saw oneself, particularly in relation to the ethical wisdom of the ancient world, and what that relationship meant for the modern individual and his society—indeed, what it meant to be modern at all.

At the end of his letter to Quintilian, Petrarch says: "I ardently desire to find you entire; and if you are anywhere in such condition, pray do not hide from me any longer. Vale" ("Opto te incolumem videre, et sicubi totus es, oro ne diutius me lateas. Vale").[17] This humanist-physician was forever barred from reassembling that Hippolytus, and thus barred from restoring his own wounds, from ending his exile from his homeland in ancient culture, because Lapo di Castiglionchio had given him only a partial manuscript. But Quintilian was "totus," "entire"; was—as Petrarch had prophetically hoped earlier in the letter—"resting intact in someone's library" ("et fortasse nunc apud aliquem totus es"). [18] He was resting, to be precise, in his entire twelve-book body in the tower of the monastery at St. Gall, outside Constance. And there he was found, and revived, in June or July of 1416, one afternoon, by Poggio Bracciolini and two friends.

With Poggio, the second phase of our inquiry, and the second generation of Italian humanism, can be said to begin. Poggio (1380– 1459), native of Arezzo, student of Salutati, who had studied with Petrarch, served the papacy as apostolic secretary for fifty years, would be chancellor of Florence at the end of his life, learned, acerb, shrewd, was one of the great discoverers of lost manuscripts in the Renaissance. Some of his greatest finds came when he was attending the Council of Constance in 1416. [19] There he and his friends made four sallies to search for pagan texts while the Church was convulsed in disputes. On the second trip, in the tower of St. Gall, Poggio found Books I–IV of the *Argonautica* of Valerius Flaccus, commentary on five orations of Cicero, and all of Quintilian. Like America, Quintilian whole had been known to others since Petrarch; but like Columbus, Poggio gets credit for the find because he knew how to publicize the discovery. Poggio immediately wrote his learned friend and fellow bibliophile, Niccolò de Niccolis in Florence, and the letter circulated. On 15 September 1416, a former and future chancellor of Florence, Leonardo Bruni, having read of Poggio's finds, wrote him from Florence in ecstatic terms:

> Vtque Camillus secundus a romulo conditor dictus est: qui ille statuit urbem. hic amissam restituit. Sic tu omnium quae iam amissa: tua virtute ac diligentia nobis restituta fuerint secundus auctor: merito nuncupabere.

> Just as Camillus was called a second founder of Rome after Romulus, who established the city, while Camillus restored it after it was lost, so you will deservedly be called the second author of all the works which were once lost and now returned to us by your integrity and diligence. [20]

Here the references to being the "second founder," "second author," carry the pride and pleasure of rediscovery, and not—as they would

have earlier, and might later—a note of melancholy at being derivative of that which remained just beyond reach. Here, the pride and
confidence of early humanism asserts itself; and why not? The promise of a return to former glory, and indeed a surpassing new glory,
seemed at hand. Bruni then turns to specific concerns:

> Quintilianus enim prius lacer: atque discerptus cuncta membra sua
> per te recuperabit. Vidi enim capita librorum Totus est: cum uix
> nobis media pars & ea ipsa lacera superesset.

> For Quintilian, who used to be mangled and in pieces, will recover all
> his parts through you. I have seen the headings of the chapters; he is
> whole, while we used to have only the middle section and that in-
> complete.[21]

And then he addresses Quintilian directly:

> O lucrum ingens. O insperatum gaudium. Ego te o Marce Fabi totum
> integrumque aspiciam. Et quanti tu mihi nunc eris: quem ego qua-
> muis lacerum crudeliter ora: Ora manusque ambas: populataque
> tempora raptis Auribus: & truncas inhonesto uulnere nares. Tamen
> propter decorem tuum in deliciis habebam.

> Oh wondrous treasure! Oh unexpected joy! Shall I see you, Marcus
> Fabius, whole and undamaged, and how much will you mean to me
> now? For I loved you even when you were cruelly deprived of your
> mouth, of your mouth and both your hands, when you were "spoiled of
> your nose and shorten'd of your ears"; still I loved you for your grace.[22]

The language of mutilation and wholeness is reminiscent of the
figures of Petrarch. Yet it derives more immediately from Poggio.
For Poggio doubtless used to Niccolò de Niccolis the same language
he uses on 15 December 1416 when he writes from Constance to
Guarino da Verona. First he extols language to Guarino in classic
humanist fashion as that which alone

> nos utentes ad exprimendam animi virtutem, ab reliquis animantibus
> segregamur. Permagna igitur habenda est gratia tum reliquarum lib-
> eralium artium inventoribus, tum vel praecipue iis, qui dicendi
> praecepta, et normam quandam perfecte loquendi suo studio, et dili-

gentia nobis tradiderunt. Effecerunt enim, ut qua in re homines caeteris animantibus maxime praestant, nos ipsos etiam homines antecelleremus.

we use to express the power of our mind and which separates us from the other beings. And so we must be deeply grateful to the pioneers in the other liberal arts and especially those who by their concern and efforts have given us rules for speaking and a pattern of perfection. They have made it possible for us to excel other men in the ability in which all men excel beasts.[23]

This celebration of rhetoric and the power of speech as the formative energy in human affairs—what Petrarch had praised in his letter— leads naturally to the greatest rhetorician and trainer of orators, Quintilian. He alone—even without Cicero—could have taught us all we needed to know of oratory. But among us Italians, says Poggio, "Quintilian was to be had only in such a mangled and mutilated state (the fault of the times, I think), that neither the figure nor the face of the man was to be distinguished in him" ("Is vero apud nos antea, Italos dico, ita laceratus erat, ita circumcisus, culpa, ut opinor, temporum, ut nulla forma, nullus habitus hominis in eo recognosceretur").[24] So far, in the adjectives and the allusion to time, Poggio says immediately, "So far you have seen the man only thus" ("Tute hominem vidisti hactenus"),[25] and cites *Aeneid* VI.495–98:

> Atque hic Priamiden laniatum corpore toto
> Deiphobum vidit, lacerum crudeliter ora,
> ora manusque ambas, populataque tempora raptis
> auribus et truncas inhonesto volnere naris.

>   his whole frame mangled
> His face cruelly torn, his face and either hand,
> His ears wrenched from despoiled brows, and
> His nostrils lopped by a shameful wound.[26]

This is the Virgilian passage about Deiphobus, one of those passages latent in Petrarch's use of the word "lacer." Thus, beneath the imagery of fragments—applied to Quintilian—we get an actual instance—in the Virgilian reminiscences—of the way humanists would handle and reintegrate fragments for their own purposes. We have humanist texts talking about reassembling Quintilian on one level, and the same texts fragmenting and reintegrating Virgil on another level—enacting what they talk about. Again, we see the process of aggression and accommodation toward antiquity that we saw in the notion of exile—a constant longing for origins that serves to allow the humanist the distance to make himself over into something like an original.

Poggio is the master of this method. After the allusion to Deiphobus mangled, he tells how he found the actual Quintilian text, now figured as a man in prison: he speaks of the squalor of his jail, the cruelty of his jailers, and describes Quintilian "with ragged beard, with hair matted with blood" ("squalentem barbam et concretos sanguine crinis"),[27] this time alluding to Aeneid II.277, where the figure of Hector appears to Aeneas in a dream before the sack of Troy.

All of these mangled Virgilian heroes, Hector, Deiphobus, Euryalus, tend to link the massive weight and authority of the Aeneid to the humanist enterprise, and tend to imply that the humanist enterprise, like the Aeneid itself, is a celebration of the way limbs, or a people dispersed, like the Trojans, may be brought home—home to Italy where, like Hippolytus, they live out their lives whole, healthy, and secure. The progress in the Aeneid of Aeneas himself, from exiled individual to restored institution, becomes another analogue to the romance of early humanism, the hope for restoration: restoration of humanists to the ancients, of ancient texts to Italy.

Indeed, this much Poggio implies in a passage separating the two Virgilian allusions: we should congratulate ourselves, he says, that "he [Quintilian] has now been restored to us in his original appearance and grandeur, whole and in perfect condition" ("cum sit in pristinum habitum et dignitatem, in antiquam formam, atque integram valetudinem . . . restitutus").[28] The thrust is still to find origins, but where Petrarch wanted to go back across distance to Rome, Poggio will bring Romans across the distance to home:

Nam si Marcus Tullius magnum praesefert gaudium pro Marco Mar-
cello restituto ab exilio, et eo quidem tempore, quo Romae plures
erant Marcelli similes, domi, forisque egregii, ac praestantes viri, quid
nunc agere docti homines debent, et praesertim studiosi eloquentiae,
cum singulare, et unicum lumen Romani nominis, quo extincto nihil
praeter Ciceronem supererat, et eum modo simili lacerum, ac dispersum, non tantum ab exilio, sed ab ipso paene interitu revocaverimus?

For if Marcus Tullius rejoiced so fervently when Marcus Marcellus was
returned from exile, and that at a time when Rome had a great many
able and outstanding men like Marcellus both at home and abroad,
what should men do now in learned circles, and especially men who
devote themselves to oratory, when the one and only light of the
Roman name, except for whom there was no one but Cicero and he
likewise cut to pieces and scattered, has through our efforts been called
back not only from exile but from almost complete destruction?[29]

For the exiled Petrarch, return was only a hope; for Poggio, the
return of the exiled ancients is a fact. In this reversal of the basic
image, we sense the massive confidence acquired by humanism in two
generations: they now know the tide flows toward them; they know
they are Aesculapiuses who can restore lacerated heroes, and bring
them to Italian woods, and incorporate the potent ethical virtues of
those heroes into their civic institutions. Poggio has no doubt the
fragments are whole, their exile is over.

Nor does another of his correspondents—the last we will consider—
have any doubts. Indeed, that writer—Francesco Barbaro, a distinguished Venetian humanist—congratulates Poggio on his discoveries
in terms that bring to the full light of consciousness the images I have
mentioned. Barbaro writes to Poggio on 6 July 1417—about a year
after the whole series of discoveries. He praises the apostolic secretary
for "releasing the monuments of literature from darkness into light"
("ut monumenta litterarum e tenebris in lucem erueres")[30]—the
imagery for history is beginning to acquire the Dark Ages / New
Dawn antithesis so familiar, alas, to us. Then:

Tu Tertullianum, tu M. Fabium Quintilianum, tu Q. Asconium
Pedianum, tu Lucretium, Silium Italicum, Marcellinum, tu Manilium

Astronomum, Lucium Septimium, Valerium Flaccum, tu Caprum, Eutychium, Probum Grammaticos, tu complures alios, Bartholomaeo collega tuo adjutore, vel fato functos vita donastis, vel longo, ut ajunt, postliminio in Latium reduxistis.

You and your helpful companion Bartholomeus have endowed Tertullian with life, and M. Fabius Quintilian, Q. Asconius Pedianus, Lucretius, Silius Italicus, Marcellinus, Manilius the astronomer, Lucius Septimus, Valerius Flaccus; you have revived the grammarians Caprus, Eutychius, and Probus, and many others who had suffered a like fate, or you have brought them back to Latium from a long absence.[31]

The metaphors are of resuscitation and return from exile, and the result is that all the gods are home.

Then Barbaro praises Poggio by reminding him of Lycurgus, who "was the first to bring back whole to Greece from Asia the work of Homer scattered in bits in various places" ("cum primus Homerum variis in locis per frustra dispersum . . . ex Asia totum Graeciam reportasset")[32] and this, by now, traditional language of fragments— following on the image of exile—leads Barbaro to the figure that I believe has been present by implication ever since Petrarch first looked upon the mutilated corpus of Quintilian:

Aesculapium inter Deos relatum accepimus, propterea quod cum alios nonnullos, tum Hippolytum supremum vitae diem functum, aliquot tamen post annos moriturum, ab inferis revocavit. Cui si populi, nationes, provinciae sacras aedes dicaverunt, quid vobis, nisi haec consuetudo jampridem obsolevisset, faciendum putarem? qui tot illustres, ac sapientissimos viros mortuos in perpetuum resuscitastis, quorum ingeniis, ac institutis non solum nos, sed etiam posteri bene dicere & honeste vivere poterunt.

We accept Aesculapius as belonging among the gods because he called back Hippolytus, as well as others from the underworld, when he had reached the day fixed as the last of his life, and thus allowed him [Hippolytus] to die only some years later. If peoples, nations, and provinces have dedicated shrines to him, what might I think ought to be done for you, if that custom had not already been forgotten? You have revived so many illustrious men and such wise men, who were dead for eternity, through whose minds and teachings not only we but our descendants will be able to live well and honorably.[33]

Now not a single text but a series of texts, not one mangled Hippolytus but a pantheon of Hippolyti, have been revived and brought home. (Barbaro adds to the myth the idea that Aesculapius refashioned not only Hippolytus but "others" as well, to accommodate his paradigm to the actual series of books discovered by Poggio.) And from this act of restoration, this successful ending to the romance of early humanism, Barbaro draws the proper humanistic conclusion: this act is not only glorious in itself, but, and this has been implicit in the figure of Aesculapius all along, the curative and healing powers of the restored bodies of work will pass into the new culture, to subsequent generations. This view of ancient virtue, once whole, now infused, is the essence of the humanist vision. It was adumbrated in Petrarch's exile who imitated the virtue of the ancient heroes, and thus found a home; it rings out in a glorious period as Barbaro, finishing another figure of praise for Poggio—the commander who has liberated those beseiged—says:

Sic humanitatem, & disciplinam, quae ad bene beateque vivendum, & ornate dicendum accommodatae sunt, non modo privatis rationibus, sed urbibus, nationibus, universis denique hominibus non mediocres utilitates afferre posse dubitandum non est.

There must be no doubt that culture and mental training which are adapted to a good and blessed life and fair speech, can bring no trifling advantages not only to private concerns but to cities, nations, and finally to all mankind.[34]

The relation of private impulse and public good, the ethically educated regard of the one for the many, is the goal of the whole humanist movement, particularly as interpreted by those whose native city was, as for Barbaro, the Venetian or, as for Poggio, the Florentine Republic.

We have seen what in Petrarch was a sense of exile and a perception of fragmentation become in Poggio and his friends a triumphant image of return and conviction of integrity. There remains one last text for us to examine in the light of our Aesculapian concerns, one last document where we can see early Renaissance humanism asserting its self-consciousness. It falls, in time, between Petrarch and Poggio. I refer to Giovanni Boccaccio's preface to his massive *Genealogia Deorum Gentilium*, the *Genealogy of the Gods*, which occupied the last thirty years of his life, from the 1340s almost until his death, a year after his beloved Petrarch, in 1375. The *Genealogia* is an encyclopedic work on myth—on the nature, relationship and meaning of the gods of the Gentiles—and it stands like Janus at the threshold of the new era, looking back at ancient treatises on the gods, like Cicero's *De Natura Deorum*, and Hyginus' *Fables*, and Fulgentius' sixth century *Mythologiae*. Boccaccio's huge work gathers in all that flows from ancient treatises and writers, from Church Father and Christian poet, and then circulates its lore through later writers, providing in its medieval format an overwhelming image of Renaissance eclecticism. The book is, like its author, learned, human, genial, devout; though also like its author it is not a little redundant, too pleased with its own efforts at times, too deferential before authorities like Petrarch and others. This splendid monster, like something from the past, could never have been produced in the past; not only is it written by a man who has tried to learn Greek, who is aware of the latest discoveries of the day, but it exudes, in its very syncretism, the spirit of revival and restoration we have spoken of—although in its own particular way as a massive prose epic, a work in many ways comparable to the great epics and romances in verse produced by poets from Pulci to Milton, save that the subject now is not the death lament of some chivalric past or the loss of some paradisiacal beginning, but a song of revival, a huge hymn to ancient culture, now restored.

We catch these notes in his preface, which Boccaccio writes in the form of a dialogue between himself and one Donino, emissary of Hugo IV, King of Cyprus and Jerusalem, who had commissioned the work but died in 1359, well before it was completed—though that seemed to bother neither Boccaccio nor his book, both author and subject swelling to fullness, rushing on, one king more or less a mere speck on the landscape. Can it be done? asks Boccaccio.

> Equidem si prestent montes faciles transitus: & solitudines inuie apertum notumque iter. Si flumina uada: & maria tranquillas undas: ac transfretanti emittat ab antro Aeolus uentos tam ualidos quam secundos: & quod maius est: sint Argiphontis talaria aurea uolucri cuicumque homini alligata pedibus: & pro uotis quocumque libuerit euolet: uix tam longos terrarum marisque tractus. etiam si illi prestetur permaxima seculorum annositas ne dum aliud agat: solum poterit peragrasse.

> Doubtless—if mountains offer easy passage and trackless deserts an open and travelled road; if rivers are fordable and seas tranquil; if Aeolus from his cave sends me in my course strong and favorable winds; or, better still, if a man might have on his feet the golden sandals of Argeiphontes, to fly whithersoever he pleased for the asking. Hardly then could he cover such extent of land and sea, though his life were never so long, and he did nothing else.[35]

Certainly it can be done, says Boccaccio—by an epic hero. But beneath the epic impulse, here presented obliquely, of the author-hero, is the view of antiquity, its myths and writers, as a landscape, a vast, difficult terrain to be sure, but a landscape that is, with good fortune and great heart, chartable, knowable. For Boccaccio, antiquity is not a distant shore—as it was for lonely, riven Petrarch; to the more robust, less tentative Boccaccio, it is a new world, fabulous but now available. Boccaccio is coy; to handle those languages and people, it will take someone, he says, "strong enough, keen enough, and with good enough memory, first to observe what is relevant, then to understand it, retain it, note it down, and finally reduce it to order" ("tam solide: tam perspicax ingenium: tamque tenax memoria: ut omnia queat uidere apposita: & intelligere uisa: & intellecta seruare: & demum calamo etiam exarare: & in opus collecta deducere").[36] He suggests Petrarch. Donino sidesteps gracefully. When Boccaccio is at last persuaded, he addresses his patron, King Hugo. He will take his frail bark to sea: "I may trace every shore and traverse every mountain grove; I may, if need be, explore

dyke and den afoot, descend even to hell, or, like another Daedalus,
go winging to the ether" ("Si omnia legero littora & montuosa etiam
nemora: scrobes & antra: si opus sit peragrauero pedibus: ad in-
feros usque descendere & Dedalus alter factus: ad aethera trans-
uolauero undique").[37] The epic hero, and his labor, are launched:
Aeneas, St. Paul, Dante—all are caught up in this epic opening. And
what will our hero find? In his words immediately following, we hear
the familiar humanist accent:

> Non aliter quam si per uastum litus ingentis naufragii fragmenta
> colligerem: sparsas per infinita poene uolumina deorum gentilium
> reliquas colligam: quas comperiam: & collectas euo diminutas at-
> que semessas & fere attritas in unum genealogie corpus: quo potero
> ordine . . . redigam.

> Everywhere . . . I will find and gather, like fragments of a mighty
> wreck strewn on some vast shore, the relics of the Gentile gods. These
> relics, scattered through almost infinite volumes, shrunk with age,
> half consumed, well-nigh a blank, I will bring into such single
> genealogical order as I can.[38]

There is the deep preoccupation with assembling the fragments of
antiquity and recreating an original shape, the shape of "genealogical
order," or "in unum genealogie corpus." Genealogy is humanist
philology writ large, the probing for the past, the translation of
significance to the present, on an epic scale. That will be Boccaccio's
great voyage, a journey of discovery which is a labor of recovery.

Now not a single lacerated text, nor a series of texts, but rather
"almost infinite volumes" confront the humanist, his new book,
made up of all these old books, will not "have a body [*corpus*] of
perfect proportion. It will, alas, be maimed—not, I hope, in too
many members—and for reasons aforesaid distorted, shrunken, and
warped" ("corpus huiusmodi habere perfectum. multum quippe: &
utinam non membrorum plurium & fortasse distortum seu con-
tractum gibbosumque habendum est. Iam rationibus premonstra-
tis").[39] His book, finished, will look like all the fragments it has
absorbed and reassembled, and so be a true copy of the originals.

Boccaccio's implication is that his book will be an original of its own kind, in which the king will see

> preter artificium fingentium poetarum & futilium deorum consan-
> guinitates & affinitates explicitas: naturalia quedam uidebis tanto
> occultata misterio ut mireris: sic & procerum gesta moresque non per
> omne trivium euagantia.

> not only the art of the ancient poets, and the consanguinity and
> relations of the false gods, but certain natural truths, hidden with an
> art that will surprise you, together with deeds and moral civilization of
> the Ancients that are not a matter of every-day information.[40]

As the plan of the book is new, so is the content. This is as close as early humanists ever come or could come to saying they were original.

Boccaccio concludes: do not be surprised at discrepancies, false-hoods, contradictions. They belong to the ancients, not to me. "Satis enim mihi erit comperta rescribere"—"I will be satisfied only to write down [write again] what is found." The humanist epic consists in "rescribere," in rewriting or reassembling in language, what the mind of man has found. Like Apollo's son, who would heal, but not judge, the scattered limbs, the early humanist revives the past; only later generations would criticize. Not now. So, before his final prayer to God for aid, Boccaccio summons in full the image for his effort, for the effort of all of them, that he has twice touched on:

> Satis aduertere possum quid mihi faciendum sit: qui inter fragosa
> uetustatis aspreta & aculeos odiorum membratim discerptum attri-
> tum & in cineres fere redactum ingens olim corpus deorum pro-
> cerumque gentilium nunc huc nunc illuc collecturus: & quasi escula-
> pius alter ad instar hippolyti consolidaturus sum.

> I can quite realize this labor to which I am committed—this vast
> system of gentile gods and their progeny, torn limb from limb
> [membratim discerptum: Petrarch's word, Virgil's word] and scattered
> among the rough and desert places of antiquity and the thorns of hate,
> wasted away, sunk almost to ashes; and here am I setting forth to
> collect these fragments, hither and yon, and fit them together, like
> another Aesculapius restoring Hippolytus.[41]

From Petrarch gazing at the mutilated body of one old book, through the whole—entire—bodies of Poggio's books by way of the mighty corpus of Boccaccio's new book, made of the limbs of the old, the humanist has implicitly or overtly seen himself as physician-restorer. But the early humanist is also Hippolytus, for as he re-assembles the past, he assembles himself. The humanist's supreme creation is finally his own sense of himself; his crucial composition is the reconstitution of self out of what the past has given him—a sense of self that is defined by the activity of making up the self. The humanist is Aesculapius to his own Hippolytus, restorer of himself out of the fragments old and new of his own humanity.

We remember that in the seminal account of Hippolytus in Book VII of the *Aeneid*, Virgil tells us that when Hippolytus was made whole, he went to live "in silvis italis," and was called "Virbius," as his son was called after him. Virbius, of course, means "twice man"—man a second time, man as he is reborn.[42] Let that finally be our emblem for the early humanist—the man made again, whole, assembled out of the fragments of his own past; the humanist, one who, by a sense of loss that is also an effort of historical imagination, has made himself up, his essential self both derivative and integrated; his consciousness old but very new; a scholar confident that, in his Italian woods, his exile is finally over and the Rome he so longed for is again alive.

3

Headlong Horses, Headless Horsemen: An Essay on the Chivalric Epics of Pulci, Boiardo, and Ariosto

Near the middle of the third *Georgic*, Virgil offers images of the power of sexual passion. One of the most striking is the horse whose whole body trembles at the familiar scent:

> ac neque eos iam frena virum neque verbera saeva,
> non scopuli rupesque cavae atque obiecta retardant
> flumina correptosque unda torquentia montis. [1]

[III.252–54]

No longer now can the rider's rein or the cruel lash stay his course, nor rocks and hollow cliffs, nay, nor opposing rivers, that tear up mountains and hurl them down the wave.

The unchecked horse is the very principle of release, more powerful even than Nature at her most elemental. Because no curb can control him, he is Nature become unnatural, potency turned monstrous, as is made clear later, in the lines on the frenzied mares and their mysterious droppings—the "hippomanes," or horse madness, favored by witches (ll. 266–83). Yet, though these images of fertility run riot, the poet is able to establish images of restraint and instances of his own control. The figure of the unchecked horse allows Virgil to show how, like the farmer, he must impose limits in order to foster growth—else without art, Nature will die of her unchecked impulse. Restraint and release, and all they mean for each other, are the essence of the image, as well as of the *Georgics*. [2]

33

Throughout the *Aeneid*, Virgil uses the metaphor of curbing, sometimes, as with Aeolus, who curbs the winds (I.54) or Dido, who will check the proud (I.523), without any extended implications. More interesting resonances occur at IV.135, where Dido's horse, resplendent in purple and gold, awaits her "ac frena ferox spumantia mandit" ("and fiercely champs the foaming bit"), the horse prefiguring the passion that will run unchecked after the episode in the cave thirty lines later. The madness here implicit in the barely restrained horse is explicitly exploited in Book XI. There, at the battle outside Latium, the Trojans push the Latins back to their city walls. The gates are closed. Some roll in trenches, "immissis pars caeca et concita frenis / arietat in portas et duros obice postis" ("some, charging blindly with loosened rein, batter at the gates and stoutly barred doors," ll. 889–90). Out of this Latin self-destruction will eventually come a strain of Roman self-sacrifice, but at this moment blindness and madness are all we see in those who smash into their own locked gates.

However, the most potent image for frenzy and restraint in the poem occurs in Book VI. Aeneas and his men approach the Sibyl. She first goads him into prayer, and then, possessed and shaking, she tries, says the poet, to loose Apollo from her breast.

> tanto magis ille fatigat
> os rabidum, fera corda domans, fingitque premendo.
>
> [VI.79–80]

> so much the more he tires her raving mouth,
> tames her wild heart, and moulds her by constraint.

Apollo rides her like a horse; and after his message is chanted through her, the poet returns to the image again: "ea frena furenti / concutit et stimulos sub pectore vertit Apollo" ("so does Apollo shake the reins as she rages, and ply the spur beneath her breast," ll. 100–01).

The Sibyl as horse, Apollo as rider, is the most telling image for the relation of *furor* (l. 102) and *frenum*—that is, for the way energy is concentrated or significance compounded through restraint. And, like the image of the horse in *Georgic III*, this one of the Sibyl and her divine rider is finally important because of the connection it establishes between the events described in the poem and the poet's activity. Here again the imposition of limit releases truth, as Apollo "fingit premendo," fashions or shapes her by restraint, just as the poet fashions his work of art by the laws of his craft. Whether reining in a horse in order to capture a pace, or disciplining the imagination in order to shape a work of art, the process is the same.

In the Sibyl and Apollo as horse and rider, there is another dimension as well. Energy comes from below, to be controlled by the higher part. This notion may go back to the centaur, our earliest image of the combined horse and rider, certainly our earliest of the power of the beast and the rationality of man.[3] The conjunction of beast and man, of energy and reason, as embodied in the centaur, is expressed through the image of Apollo riding the Sibyl, save that now god and man, not man and beast, are joined. Now on the vertical scale established by the image, what was bestial is human; what was human is divine. The image of the horse and rider has tremendous flexibility.

In his *Consolatio Philosophiae*, Boethius returns several times to the imagery of riding, specifically of curbing, always at crucial points in the book. In the eighth poem of Book II, on how love is the ruling principle of the universe, he says that if Love loosened the reins, then all now bound would make perpetual war:

> Hic si frena remiserat,
> Quidquid nunc amat inuicem
> Bellum continuo geret . . .[4]

The Universe, says Boethius, is bound into freedom by love—as again the paradox of meaningful release as a function of restraint is exploited in the image of the curbed horse. He makes the point again in the second poem of Book III: "Quantas rerum flectat habenas / Natura potens" ("how mighty Nature guides the reins of all things"), and at the end returns once again to the image to show that nothing is outside of God's plan: "Sic quae permissis fluitare uidetur habenis, / Fors patitur frenos ipsaque lege meat" ("Chance, too, which seems to rush along with slack reins, is bridled and governed by law"—Book V, poem 1). Boethius uses the imagery of reins and curbing to underscore the great theme of his book, which is the expansion of spiritual freedom because of the limits of Providence. But Boethius does more—he invests the imagery with a moral energy, a spiritual immediacy, that guarantees the life of the image after him.

Dante exploits the same imagery to great effect. In the *Convivio* (IV.xvii.4), for instance, we read of Temperance, "che è regola e freno de la nostra gulositade" ("which is the rule and rein on our gluttony").[5] Perhaps the most interesting example, however, occurs early in Book IV, where

> lo Imperadore . . . sia lo cavalcatore de la umana volontade. Lo quale cavallo come vada sanza lo cavalcatore per lo camp assai è manifesto, e spezialmente ne la misera Italia, che sanza mezzo alcuno a la sua governazione è rimasa. [*Convivio* IV.ix.10][6]

> the Emperor . . . is the rider of the human will. And how that horse goes without the rider over the field is most obvious, and especially in miserable Italy, that is left without means for its governance.

Regardless of how the image is finally translated—whether Italy, or the Emperor, or the horse of the human will is referred to by the *sua* preceding *governazione*—the vision of the streaking, unchecked horse is an unforgettable metaphor for appetite run wild, a people completely leaderless.

In the *Commedia*, the image of the *freno*, the curb, is used fourteen times, once in the *Inferno* (for Phaeton, XVII.107), once in the *Paradiso* (for Adam, another Phaeton, VII.26), and twelve times in the *Purgatorio*. These usages in the *Purgatorio* exploit every dimension—physical, ethical, and spiritual—of the image, and are appropriate to the *cantica* that is precisely about release through restraint. However, I would like to touch briefly on another passage where the image is used in a different way:

> Allor mi dolsi, e ora mi ridoglio
>   quando drizzo la mente a ciò ch'io vidi,
>   e più lo 'ngegno affreno ch'i' non soglio,

perché non corra che virtù nol guidi;
sì che, se stella bona o miglior cosa
m'ha dato 'l ben, ch'io stessi nol m'invidi.

[*Inferno* XXVI. 19–24][7]

The grief that seized me then I feel anew
When I recall the sight that met my eyes;
Remembering, I keep tighter rein on wit
Than is my wont, lest it may run unchecked
By virtue's guidance, so that if perchance
Some favoring star or nobler arbiter
Has blessed me with a talent, I myself
May not pervert it to my own dismay.

Here, in his own voice, the poet sets up the crucial difference between himself as poet (and by extension in the episode proper, as pilgrim) and that other great voyager, Ulysses. As the canto unfolds, we see how, for all the similarities between them, Dante is distinct from Ulysses; for the poet has restrained his imaginative power to remain within God's (and virtue's) plan, whereas Ulysses has released the full force of his rhetorical power and, a Siren to his crew, has led his men away from reason's dictates. Dante restrains his "ingegno" so as not to deny himself its good; Ulysses releases his, without restraint, and loses all. Dante the poet shapes his utterance and thus shapes his moral being, figured in the pilgrim, whereas Ulysses misshapes his language in order to persuade and thus misshapes his men.

We see this process even more clearly when, at the end of the *Purgatorio*, Dante returns to the image. The mountain has been scaled, and the garden and its rivers passed through. If he had more space, he says, he would write of the sweet draughts that never satisfy:

ma perché piene son tutte le carte
ordite a questa cantica seconda,
non mi lascia più ir lo fren de l'arte.

[*Purgatorio* XXXIII. 139–41]

But inasmuch as all the sheets ordained
For this my second Canticle are filled,
The curb of art lets me no further go.

The curb applied *by* Dante in *Inferno* XXVI is applied *to* Dante in *Purgatorio* XXXIII. The change is significant, for the pilgrim has just achieved his greatest earthly freedom in the garden and, *rifatto* (*Purgatorio* XXXIII.143), now ascends to Paradise, a release that is precisely the result of restraints he has assumed to perfect his moral being. Dante shows us how to curb in order to create, that is, he gives us an insight into the aesthetic process he is engaged in. But the aesthetic shaping is also, for Dante, a moral shaping: the poet shaping his pilgrim, God, his poet. And each creator (Dante or God) refrains his creature (pilgrim or poet) in order to reform him. The aesthetic and the moral are united in the imagery of curbing.

Dante has greatly extended the implications of Virgil's "fingit premendo" (*Aeneid* VI.80), Apollo's shaping the Sibyl by constraining her, as if she were clay and he were a sculptor. Dante has moralized this figure, and has brought out the latent self-consciousness in the riding image—the sense that, as a man refrains his horse, so he guides himself. The poets of the Renaissance epic, therefore, could find the multiple images of curbing a horse, loosing a horse, and riding in harmony, exploited in their ethical, moral and aesthetic dimensions by their great predecessors in the epic tradition. These are images that Pulci, Boiardo and Ariosto would return to often, for there is no figure more central to chivalric epic than the checked or unchecked horse and its rider. Nor is there a more apt image for the effort the epic poet is engaged in.

LUIGI PULCI, *Morgante*[8]

In Canto XIII of the *Morgante*, Rinaldo comes to the court of King Marsilio. Suddenly a messenger appears and, falling to his knees, recounts the following:

> che morte ha cinquecento o più persone
> un gran caval co' denti e colle penne,
> ch'era sfrenato, e fu già di Gisberto,
> e pareva un demòn là in un diserto.

[st. 51]

> that five hundred or more people have been killed
> by a great horse with teeth and plumes
> that was unchecked, and came of Gisberto,
> and seemed a demon there in the desert.

The horse is a symbol for the part of man we must govern most wisely. But even more, it represents the energy in life most dangerous to the established chivalric conventions and norms. We see this most clearly when Rinaldo sets his noble mount Baiardo to combat with the mad and wild horse. In the process, Rinaldo sets up an image of the two ways life can run—into pattern or sheer energy, into convention and containment or vital deformity and death. He sets up the dialectic that informs the *Morgante*. He also creates an image of the gap between the ideal and the actual; and in that gap the poem will reside.

Rinaldo watches the fight between the palfrey and the marauder for two hours. Then two stanzas sum up the episode, and much of the poem:

> Rinaldo un poco stette a vedere;
> ma poi, veggendo che 'l giuoco pur basta,
> e che co' morsi quel bravo destriere
> e colle zampe Baiardo suo guasta,
> dispose fare un colpo a suo piacere;
> détto a quell' altro un pugno tra gli orecchi
> col guanto, tal che non ne vuol parecchi;
>
> e cadde come e' fussi tramortito.
> Baiardo si scostò, ch'ebbe paura.
> Gran pezzo stette il cavallo stordito;
> poi si riebbe, e tutto s'assicura.
> Rinaldo verso lui presto fu gito,
> prese la bocca alla mascella dura,
> missegli un morso ch'aveva recato;
> e quel cavallo umile è diventato.
>
> [XIII.64–65]

> Rinaldo sat awhile to watch;
> but then, seeing the game had gone far enough,
> and that with bites and hooves

> that big horse was smashing up his Baiardo,
> he resolved to strike a blow in his favor.
> And while Baiardo was reeling,
> he gave that other a fist between the ears
> with his glove—such as few would want;
>
> and it fell as if it had fainted.
> Baiardo ran to one side, he was afraid.
> For a good while the horse lay stunned,
> then it recovered and checked himself over.
> Rinaldo quickly went to him,
> took his mouth by the hard jaw,
> put in a bit he had brought,
> and that horse became docile.

As the wild thing is killing Baiardo, the chivalric fiction, Rinaldo does what Pulci will always see man as having to do: he uses his hands to reshape the situation. We must respond to actualities, as events occur, says Pulci, and not trust to conventions or codes to do our living for us. Of course, every new adjustment, every insertion of the self into the maelstrom of events, creates, potentially, a new convention, a new pattern for behavior; but to understand this dialectic is to understand the game that is life. Here Rinaldo knows when his particular *gioco* (64) has gone far enough; we will see later how Pulci sees all existence in this fashion. Now, the wild horse has sufficiently threatened the order of things so that the order must be made to include him if it and we are to survive.

The horse is stunned by a blow from the mailed fist. Why not sooner? After all, five hundred have died. The answer is that Pulci, like all Renaissance writers, is interested in paradigms for behavior, not in continuous narrative realism. And after the mailed fist, the process of *frenare*, of curbing, begins. It is done by hand, by the shaping power of the human, the higher part fashioning out of the energy of the lower something that transforms them both: "fingit premendo." The wild horse becomes a *pecorin*, a *pecorella* ("lamb")—in both cases a *maraviglia* ("wonder," at 66, 68)—and finally a symbol for the love between Rinaldo and Marsilio's daughter Luciana

(68–69). From the stuff of murderous chaos, Rinaldo has wrought something quite new.

The episode of Rinaldo and the "cavallo sfrenato" encompasses a good deal of Pulci's manner and meaning. I intend to look briefly at two specific parts of the climax of the episode as a way of glimpsing some of the larger issues in the *Morgante*. First, let us return to the stunned horse: "e cadde come e' fussi tramortito" ("and it fell as if it had fainted," 65). The image of the supine horse is a constant in the poem, always associated with ghastly carnage. For instance, at the battle around Paris, the Christians are hemmed in by death:

> l'un sopra l'altro morto era caduto,
> e gli uomini e' cavalli attraversati,
> tal che miracol sarebbe tenuto
> quanti furon poi morti annumerati.
> Avea cinque ore o più già combattuto:
> or pensi ognun quanti e' n'abbi schiacciati.
>
> [X.47]

> one on the other had fallen dead,
> and the men and horses lay across each other,
> so it would have taken a miracle
> to reckon the number of those dead.
> [They] had fought for five hours or more:
> think of how many had been squashed.

This vision of the reductiveness and anonymity of warfare is but a prefiguration of the scene at Roncesvalles. There Charlemagne sees:

> i cavalieri armati
> l'un sopra l'altro in su la terra rossa,
> gli uomini co' cavalli attraversati;
> e molti son caduti in qualche fossa,
> nel fango in terra fitti arrovesciati;
> chi mostra sanguinosa la percossa,
> chi 'l capo avea quattro braccia discosto,
> da non trovargli in Giusaffà sì tosto.
>
> [XXVII.198][9]

> the armed knights
> [lay] one on the other on the red ground,
> the men with the horses across them;
> and many had fallen in ditches,
> in the mud, rammed in the ground upside down;
> those who show a bloody wound,
> those with a head and four scattered limbs
> that won't be found in Jehoshaphat very soon.

Throughout the poem, the only natural consequence of men and horses mixed, of war, is deformity and death. And, throughout, with his savage wit, Pulci employs a striking figure for the shapelessness of men and beasts slaughtered together in battle: it is the image of the pudding or stew. In Canto VII. 56: "e' ne facean gelatine e mortiti,"[10] ("they made a pudding or stew"), and later:

> era a veder sotto questa rovina
> morti costor come una gelatina.
>
> [XIX. 173]

> there was to be seen under this ruin
> these dead as if in a pudding.

> tutta la terra pareva coperta
> di gente smizzicata saracina,
> da poter far mortito o gelatina.
>
> [XXIII. 38]

> all the ground seemed covered
> with chopped up Saracens
> as if to make a stew or pudding.

The "stew" of battle is most forcibly described at Roncesvalles, which is:

> un tegame
> dove fussi di sangue un gran mortito,
> di capi e di peducci e d'altro ossame
> un certo guazzabuglio ribollito . . .
>
> [XXVII. 56]

> a pan
> where there was a great stew of blood,
> of heads and little feet and other bones,
> a kind of boiled concoction . . .

But the stew extends beyond the battlefield; shapelessness and dissolution underlie all of life. We understand this when we hear that
splendid Tuscan word *guazzabuglio* ("concoction"), a word, we
realize, that we have heard before.

At the end of his exuberant monologue to Morgante, Margutte
compared his life to a book (XVIII.140), but to a special kind of
book:

> Io t'ho lasciato indietro un gran capitolo
> di mille altri peccati in guazzabuglio;
> ché s'i'volessi legerti ogni titolo,
> e' ti parrebbe troppo gran mescuglio.
>
> [XVIII.142]

> I left behind you a great composition
> of a thousand other sins in a concoction;
> for if I were to read you every title,
> it would strike you as too great a mixture.

As Margutte goes on to say, his life is an endless story; but his final
word will be: "che tradimento ignun non feci mai" ("I have never
betrayed anyone," 142). Morgante is delighted:

> non crederrei con ogni sua misura
> ti rifacessi appunto più natura,
> né tanto accomodato la voler mio.
>
> [143–144]

> I wouldn't have thought that Nature
> could have made you better to its own measure,
> nor better fitted to my desire.

Here is the heart of Pulci's vision: all of life and Nature is made
according to *misura*; and that measure, that perfect proportion,
resides in gluttony (see XIX.86, where "gelatina o solci" figure the

stuff of existence) and in *mescuglio* and *guazzabuglio*. Life is the process of consumption and expansion, always tending to dissolution and deformity. Food, men, horses, words—all are part of the ever-expanding, fermenting mix, the ever-decaying, ever-swelling mingle of undigested elements, physical and linguistic, that is human existence. The only *misura* is finally *mescuglio* or *guazzabuglio*—Pulci sees no check, no rein, on appetite and so he hymns deformity. He celebrates monstrosity as the only principle of proportion. Finally, of course, the book of Margutte's life—crammed with splendid sin and with joy in excess, recounted in the tough, slangy, gamey gristle of proverbial Tuscan—is only an image of the larger book. The greater *guazzabuglio*, the thicker, more redolent *mortito*, is the *Morgante* itself, constantly expanding, cannibalizing older poems, growing to twenty-three cantos, then to twenty-eight, ending only with the perception that decay outstrips even the glory of excess, and that Hell is here in our daily lives. Despite efforts of convention, of social codes and constructs, the urges in human affairs to shapelessness, to becoming a stew, seem too great to check.

And yet Pulci does assert his control. He does imply throughout that he can contain the stew, or, at least, that one can gain some perspective on a world whose proportions are so deformed. The key to this attitude, which extends throughout the poem as much as the sense of life as a *mortito* does, can also be found in the episode of the *cavallo sfrenato* with which we began. We remember that after Rinaldo had watched the wild horse batter Baiardo for two hours, "veggendo che 'l giuoco pur basta" ("seeing the game had gone far enough," XIII.64), he moved to stop the battle. Throughout the poem, battle—the cause of the shapeless stew of carnage—is also seen as a *gioco* ("game"). Over and over, the process whereby life loses its human form, the process that symbolizes the lack of form in human existence, is distanced and thus controlled by calling it a "game." The terms of the dialectic in the poem are, finally, undifferentiated confusion and decay (*mortito, mescuglio, gelatina, guazzabuglio*), and cool, skeptical formality, an acceptance of rules without any faith in them (*gioco* or *gioco netto*, or a "safe bet," a game where no risks are taken, a game everyone wants and no one has).[11]

We know that the idea of play is profoundly important to Renaissance culture; it is at the heart of Erasmus's great satire:

> And he is unseasonable who does not accommodate himself to things as they are, who is "unwilling to follow the market," who does not keep in mind at least that rule of conviviality, "Either drink or get out"; who demands, in short, that the play should no longer be a play. [*The Praise of Folly*][12]

It is the essence of the wisdom of *Don Quixote*, as we know when Montesinos tells his cousin Durandarte that Quixote has come to render them *desencantados* ("disenchanted"), and Durandarte replies that if it doesn't happen, "cuando así no sea ¡oh primo!, digo, paciencia y barajar" ("even if it doesn't happen, oh cousin, have patience and shuffle the cards," pt. 2, chap. 23).[13] Here, the losing gambler's proverb makes it clear that life is bearable only so long as the game continues, that play is so crucial because we must sustain the capacity to maintain illusion. Yet Erasmus or Cervantes, or indeed Rabelais, after all, are only the heirs of Pulci, for no one understands better, in these terms, the necessity for play in human life than Margutte. We return to the beginning of that long speech to Morgante.

> Mentre ch'io ho danar, s'io sono a giuoco,
> rispondo come amico a chiunque chiama;
> e giuoco d'ogni tempo e in ogni loco,
> tanto che al tutto e la roba e la fama
> io m'ho giucato, e' pel già della barba:
> guarda se questo pel primo ti garba.
>
> Non domandar quel ch'io so far d'un dado,
> o fiamma o traversin, testa o gattuccia,
> o lo spuntone: è va per parentado,
> ché tutti siàn d'un pelo e d'una buccia.
> E forse al camuffar ne incaco, o bado,
> o non so far la berta o la bertuccia,
> o in furba o in calca o in bestrica mi lodo?
> Io so di questo ogni malizia e frodo.
>
> [XVIII. 121–22]

When I have money, if I am playing,
I answer like a friend to whoever calls;
and I play at all times, anywhere,
so that for any and every stake
I've played, until I'm stripped:
see if being in your birthday suit pleases you.

Don't ask me if I know about dice,
about snake-eyes, trey, Little Joe from Kokomo,
boxcar or seven-out; it's in the blood;
we're all the same under the skin.
And do you think I don't give a crap about a good con,
or that I can't take anyone for a ride,
or can't play the shell game or steal your shirt?
I know every trick there is.

Play until you're skinned, says Margutte, until there is no more. The game is all in the playing, not in believing that anything will come of it. Life consists of seeing everything as a gamble, with no safe bets, a *gioco* with no *gioco netto*. It is this attitude of total tolerance and total skepticism that gives Margutte, and others, their ability to accept deformity as a norm. Thus, war or any other system is a game if one believes that fraud is the only truth and decay the only constant. Indeed, this attitude toward life can shape it, can give it form, if one is willing arbitrarily to assert that what seems only a *mortito* or *guazzabuglio* is really just another pass with the dice, another trick in the endless show. Margutte seems to speak, finally, for the poet whose poem is the largest game of all, the poet who, even later, confesses that "ch'io sono stato al monte di Sibilla, / che mi pareva alcun tempo un bel gioco" ("For I have been to the Sibyl's mountain, / which once seemed to me a good game," XXIV. 112). This is the poet who admits that magic was his favorite game, that magic and its demons were his Parnassus and his Muses (113; also XXVIII. 141). Pulci sees making magic, like writing poetry, as the final game, the willed play of the mind over the void. The dialectic in the poem, and in the poet, between the desire to believe and the inability to believe, between the perception of shape as made by the mind and immersion

in formlessness as experienced by the body, between Jehoshaphat and
Caïna, is constant.

Finally, at the end, Pulci proffers several images for release and
restraint that sum up this dialectic and its larger implications. These
images all appear together in a remarkable stanza near the close of his
poem. He is musing on the *Morgante* and its making:

> Ben so che spesso, come già Morgante,
> lasciato ho forse troppo andar la mazza;
> ma dove sia poi giudice bastante,
> materia c'è da camera e da piazza;
> ed avvien che chi usa con gigante,
> convien che se n'appicchi qualche sprazza,
> sì ch'io ho fatto con altro battaglio
> a mosca cieca o talvolta a sonaglio.
>
> [XXVIII.142]

> I know that often, just like Morgante,
> I've let things go a little too far;
> but where there is a proper judge,
> there is material for the salon and the square.
> It follows that whoever has to do with a giant
> will have to take on some of his traits,
> though I have fought other [different] battles
> at *mosca cieca* or *sonaglio* [blind man's bluff].

Lasciare or *mettere troppa mazza* means getting carried away in storytell-
ing, going too far. And here the poet is saying that, like Morgante, he
has been guilty of excess, of surpassing limit, of running unchecked.
The radical urge in the poem toward shapelessness is shaped here by a
colloquial phrase, a phrase that also occurred earlier when Pulci was
ruminating on his effort:

> e bisognòe qui andar pel segno ritto
> (non so se troppa mazza altrove misse),
> che l'aüttor che *Morgante* compose
> non direbbe bugie tra queste cose.
>
> [XXVIII.63]

It is necessary here to go on the straight line
(I don't know if it has gone too far)
so that the author who writes the *Morgante*
wouldn't tell any lies among all these things.

Again, the hint of having gone too far, the ironic worry that his magic releases lies instead of truth; but now this concern is played off against an image of restraint. "Andar pel segno ritto" refers to the carpenter's art, and to the ochre line, guiding a saw, that is made by snapping a string covered with dye against the wood. Pulci counters all the images of stews, of swelling language and imagination, of sheer size beyond measure, with a carpenter's image, an image like Rinaldo's placing the bit in the horse's mouth in Canto XIII, an image of the human hand controlling the shape of things and not relying on convention or custom to shape things for us.

The poet is literally a *fabbro*, an artisan making his momentary stays against confusion. It is an image whose power derives from its directness and plainness, and it is one that Pulci uses for his art at critical points in the poem. For instance, when he refers to one of his fictional sources, the author "Arnaldo," he speaks of him as one who "va pel fil della sinopia saldo / sanza uscir punto del segno ritto" ("goes by the straight line / without leaving at all what was marked," XXVII.80).[14] And when he speaks of his major fictional source, "Alfamennone," and the authority for the fantastic stories about Morgante, Pulci still asserts that he is following the truth: "Tanto è ch'io voglio andar pel solco ritto" ("so much do I want to follow the straight line," XIX.153). Thus, whenever Pulci refers to his art he introduces the image of control to justify precisely the release of a new story. He knows that the lies in his poem, or in life, can only be effective when they are purveyed as the truth; he knows that the horror of shapelessness is made more acute, but also more bearable, when it is given explicitly artistic form. The dialectic between restraint and release, between *misura* and *mescuglio*, is finally for Pulci a way of talking about the very effort he is engaged in—the loosing of images that must contain rather than create chaos.

For Pulci, the identification between what his characters do and what he does was firmly made at XXVIII.142, the stanza cited above, where Pulci allied himself with Morgante. There Pulci said that, like his character, he had "lasciato . . . troppo andar la mazza":

> ed avvien che chi usa con gigante,
> convien che se n'appicchi qualche sprazza,
> sì ch'io ho fatto con altro battaglio
> a mosca cieca o talvolta a sonaglio.

> It follows that whoever has to do with a giant
> will have to take on some of his traits,
> though I have fought other [different] battles
> at *mosca cieca* or *sonaglio* [blind man's bluff].

To understand this identification of poet and character, we must first know that *mosca cieca* or *sonaglio* are names for a child's game in which a player is blindfolded and cries out "Sonaglio," while the others form a circle around him and answer "Béccati quest'aglio." They then shove and hit the blindfolded player until he is able to grab one of his tormentors, who then enters the circle and takes the blindfold. This game is alluded to throughout the *Morgante* (II.11; VI.15; VII.12, 43; X.147; XXIII.38) and here at XXVIII.142. And it serves, in every case but the last, as a metaphor for battle. In short, *mosca cieca* is the specific game, the *gioco*, that underlies the concept of play and informs the poem. In the last allusion, at XXVIII.142, the game refers not only to the matter of the poem and Morgante's place in it, but also to the composition of the poem and Pulci's role as maker.

And what it means is that, much as Morgante and Pulci have both participated in and celebrated excess, much as both saw life as a game and thus, up to a point, managed to remain untouched by the inevitable decay of existence, in the end Morgante, unlike Pulci, loses at *mosca cieca*. Finally, in the absurd game the world plays with us, Morgante—massive, vital and oddly human—is killed. He is killed by a crab that bites his heel (XX.50 f.), precisely as the Tuscan proverb he once cited with a laugh says: "I granchi credon morder le balene" ("Crabs think they can bite whales," XIX.7). The power in the proverb comes to life, and loosed, it kills. But this is what Pulci has been saying all along: that any form of energy—a proverb, a wild horse, a giant, a poem—can, if let loose, destroy normal expectations, assumptions, patterns, conventions. Any game, like chivalry, or magic, or writing, can get out of hand and result in a terrible "stew" of men and horses, or in heresy, or in an aimless and shapeless poem.

And that is how he has played *mosca cieca* differently from Morgante. Pulci has not, like Morgante, celebrated excess as an end in itself but rather as a means to fullness within measure. For, while Pulci celebrates energy—never more so than when it is fully actualized—he also celebrates it only this side of having it overwhelm all limits. He is, ultimately, the poet of the thin red line. Pulci has always known when to swell the story and when to cut it on the mark. Like Rinaldo, who knew when the "cavallo sfrenato" was going too far with Baiardo, who knew the game, Pulci has known when to explode and when to contract, when to expand a literary convention and when to follow it, when to embellish the older chivalric literature and when to embody its essence.

Pulci has played *mosca cieca* with the literary tradition; but because he knew when to change the players and how to keep the game going, it has not done him in. I think the model for Pulci's view of this process, in poetry and in life, is there near the middle of his poem, in Canto XIII, where we started. There, the unchecked horse, representing all the glorious, new energies that kill older forms, is transformed by the miraculous hand of the man into a symbol of peace, the lamb, and into a figure for love between man and woman. To transform murderous power into art is the only game Pulci finally can believe in. It is what his poem does, and it is what the figure of the unchecked horse finally comes to mean.

Matteo Maria Boiardo, *Orlando Innamorato*[15]

Pulci exulted in life's excess even as he sought to shape it before it became chaos. Boiardo's view is simpler, less ambiguous, and his poem is more orderly, less given over to what it would contain, perhaps less profound. Boiardo, too, knows that life (and art) tend instinctively toward deformity, but he takes no pleasure in the energies released by decomposition; he does not hunger for, as well as recoil from, the stew of human affairs. Boiardo deeply fears the impulse in life toward dissolution. He wants a universe of purpose, perspective, and proportion and he believes he can provide at least the model for such a world in his art, in his lovely creation of glistening knights and graceful ladies.

Pulci believed the death of old conventions released energy for new ones, thus the (futile) dialectic of his vision. Boiardo is much more aristocratic and conservative. He understands the limitations of chivalry; he will note the ironic discrepancy between surface and substance, between what we say and what we do— though not with the piercing clarity of his younger contemporary, Ariosto. But Boiardo does not find anything liberating or exhilarating in the decay of order and the pursuit of excess; rather, he laments the passing of the chivalric world and, in his way, seeks to memorialize it, shortcomings and all. As we will see, his terms for life and art are very similar to Pulci's, but the final emphasis is very different, and the vision is less hectic, more refined.

The best illustration of these similarities and differences is found in Boiardo's attitudes toward love and limitation. Both the power of love and a proper sense of limit are established in the opening stanza of the poem:

> Signori e cavallier che ve adunati
> Per odir cose dilettose e nove,
> State attenti e quïeti, ed ascolatati
> La bella istoria che 'l mio canto muove;
> E vedereti i gesti smisurati,
> L'alta fatica e le mirabil prove
> Che fece il franco Orlando per amore,
> Nel tempo del re Carlo imperatore,
>
> [I.i.1]

> Lords and knights here assembled
> To hear of things delightful and new,
> Pay attention, stay quiet and listen
> To the lovely history that moves my song,
> And see the boundless deeds,
> The high labor and the wondrous efforts
> That French Orlando did for love
> In the time of King Charles the Emperor.

At the middle of the stanza are those "gesti smisurati" ("boundless deeds"), those excessive, destructive deeds that are done for love. Boiardo's great themes are, finally, the destructiveness of passion, the life-enhancing quality of cool control. Of course, he will praise love, just as he described some of Orlando's deeds as "alta fatica . . . mirabil prove." But even as love is praised, there is always the hint of something else. For instance, in the famous stanzas on love as the universally unifying force, a very ambiguous note is sounded in the last couplet.

> Ché amore il senno e lo intelletto avanza,
> Né giova al provedere arte o pensiero.
> Giovani e vecchi vanno alla sua danza,
> La bassa plebe col segnore altiero;
> Non ha remedio amore, e non la morte;
> Ciascun prende, ogni gente ed ogni sorte.
>
> [I.xxviii.2]

> For love advances good sense and intellect,
> It helps to furnish art or high thoughts,
> The young and the old move to its dance,
> [As does] the meanest plebe with the haughty lord;
> There is no remedy for love, and none for death;
> It takes everyone, every person and every destiny.

For all the splendid things love is, it is also like death, irresistible and remorseless. The stanza describes a dual perspective on love that is characteristic of the poem as a whole. One more example: later in the poem, we begin to hear an even more menacing note, one that, as we will see, resounds often in the last part of the poem.

Amor primo trovò le rime e' versi,
I suoni, i canti ed ogni melodia;
E genti istrane e populi dispersi
Congionse Amore in dolce compagnia.
Il diletto e il piacer serian sumersi,
Dove Amor non avesse signoria;
Odio crudele e dispietata guerra,
Se Amor non fusse, avrian tutta la terra.

[II.iv.2]

Love first found the rhymes and verses,
The sounds, the songs, and every melody;
And unknown people and disparate folk
Join in Love in sweet company.
The delight and the pleasure will be submerged
Where Love does not hold sway;
Cruel hate and spiteful war,
If Love is not, will conquer the earth.

Love is central to the world of the poem because it can effect so much: love can lead to high deeds or to "gesti smisurati"; it can bind society in harmony or it can falter and leave men "sommersi" ("sunk") in excess. Like Pulci, Boiardo knows that the force for life—he calls it love—can also be the agent of death, that the lovely world of proportion and purpose contains within it the potential for shapelessness, and that this potential is always just beneath the surface. But where Pulci rode out the impulse toward decay and dissolution in order to engage (and hence control) it, Boiardo, always aware of its power, hopes to check or rein it in from the very outset.

Thus, from the beginning the general instinct in everything to go beyond proper limits, to be "smisurato," is repeated as a warning, over and over. And all things participate in this instinct: Astolfo's helmet is "di valore ismesurato" ("of measureless value," I.i.61); Ferraguto "amava oltra misura" ("loved beyond measure") and later makes "un salto smisurato" ("a boundless leap," I.i.72; 78); a giant is called "Argesto smisurato" ("measureless Argesto," I.i.75), while later another, Malpresa, is "dismisurato" ("unmeasurable," III.i.59).

Later again, in the garden of Falerina, Orlando sees a tree "fuor di misura" ("beyond all measure," II.iv.48), with a harpy sitting in it: "Grandi ha le branche e smisurato artiglio" ("It had huge claws and measureless talons," 51). The creature "Turbosse oltra misura il conte Orlando" ("Disturbed Count Orlando beyond measure," 59). Characters, like Bradamante (III.v.51) or Ranaldo (I.v.5; II.xxx.12) can give blows "tanto smisurato" or "oltra misura" or "fuor d'ogni misura," while at other times whole episodes are beyond measure. For instance, Turpin tells us, says the poet, of a "bestia smisurata" ("measureless beast," II.xxviii.33); but, he continues, "Io non ho prova che chiarir vi possa, / Perché io non presi alora la misura" ("I have no way of clarifying this / Because I did not take its measure," 36).

Thus everything—objects, animals, humans, even recorded history itself—tends to excess, and despite what he says here, Boiardo is constantly engaged in taking their measure, in checking and refraining the urge to swell to shapelessness. At times, his control consists of telling us exactly what the result of this impulse to swell will be. This is the apocalyptic strain in the poem, visions of dissolution and confusion that correspond to Pulci's view of existence as a grisly stew or his invocation of Caïna. For instance, we noted above the warning that without Love and its ordering power, all would be sunk or dissolved ("sumerso," II.iv.2). This was, at that point, a warning of what was potential in human affairs. But at other points, the fear of losing a vision of harmony, of losing the capacity to assert a universe of proportion and purpose, becomes translated into a vision of actuality. The aristocrat feels the mob pressing in, and the fear of shapelessness is cosmic and real. Agramante's army passes from Africa to France:

> Chi potrebbe il tumulto racontare
> Da la gente sì strana e sì diversa,
> Che par che 'l celo e il mondo se sumersa?
>
> [II.xxviii.54][16]

> Who could tell the tumult
> Of people so strange and so diverse,
> That it seemed the heavens and earth would be sunk?

Or again:

> Or torniamo alla gente africana
> E a questi re, che al campo sono entrati
> Con tal romore e grido sì diverso,
> Che par che il celo e il mondo sia sumerso.
>
> [II.xxx.7]

> Now let us return to the African people,
> And to these kings, who have come on the field
> With such a noise and cries so diverse
> That it seems the heavens and earth will sink.

As we will see, the only diversity or differentness that Boiardo can calmly envision is that created by and in his own work of art. Otherwise his poem, in something bordering on xenophobia, warns us against diversity of any other kind. The apocalyptic visions of the cosmos drowned in barbarians, of civility losing its shape, were prophetic; for when Charles VIII brought his French armies into Italy in 1494, Boiardo evidently could no longer sustain his poem. He stopped writing his epic, leaving it unfinished; the blow to his vision of what Italy ought to be was too great to encompass in poetry.

All of Boiardo's deep fears of diversity and decay, and his equally deep desires for order, are summed up in an episode in Book II, Canto XXX. This is really one of the climactic episodes of the poem, for the third book, ten years in the making, is truncated and elegiac in tone. The scene is the great battle between the armies of Charlemagne and Agramante. Charlemagne rallies the Christians by reminding them of their divinely inspired duty, and he exhorts them not to fear the foe's greater numbers. A bit of fire can ignite a great deal of straw. Then he cries:

> Se foriosi entramo alla battaglia,
> Non sosterranno il primo assalto apena.
> Via! Loro addosso a briglie abbandonate!
> Già sono in rotta; io il vedo in veritate.
>
> [II.xxx.44]

> If we enter the battle furiously [madly]
> They will barely be able to sustain the first assault;
> Go! After them with loosened bridles!
> Already they are in ruin. I see it truly.

"A briglie abbandonate"—Charlemagne urges release, "sfrenatura," upon his cavaliers. He urges them to do precisely what the poet has been warning the reader against—to court excess as a means to restraint, expanding toward death as a way of retaining a hold on life. Boiardo's Charlemagne expresses Pulci's vision, that one asserts control by exploiting the energy of decay. Pulci urged this because he believed only in the final order of the dialectic of expansion and retraction; Boiardo's Charlemagne courts chaos because he believes in God's ordering hand. Boiardo has finally found a way of incorporating the terrifying energy (and imagery) of "sfrenatura" into his poem; and having done that, he then immediately offers a critique of what I have called Pulci's vision.

In the next stanza, Boiardo tells us what energy the language of excess releases. It is something we have seen and heard before:

> Qua se levò l'altissimo romore;
> Chi suona trombe e chi corni, e chi crida;
> Par che il cel cada e il mondo se divida.
>
> [II.xxx.45]

> Here the most intense sound arose;
> Some blew trumpets, some horns, some yelled;
> It seems that the heavens fall and the earth yawns.

Cacophony as an index of apocalypse: the same sight and sound we had in II.iv.2, II.xxvii.21, II.xxviii.54, and II.xxx.7 is here applied to the Christians moving into battle. Boiardo is saying that Charlemagne's command threatens the very order he wants to maintain. And when the Saracens stream out in vast numbers, the full force of Boiardo's critique emerges:

> Discese il campo in mezo a poco a poco,
> Fosso non vi è, né fiume, che confini,

Ma urtano insieme gli animi di foco,
Spronando per quel piano a gran tempesta;
Ruina non fu mai simile a questa.

[II.xxx.46]

The field shrinks at the middle, little by little;
There is no trench, or river, as a boundary,
But the souls in flame scream together
Spurring on that plain like a huge storm;
Ruin was never anything like this.

The battlefield shrinks as the armies move toward each other, but compression is an illusion. The reality is ghastly expansion, beyond all limits, either man-made (trenches) or natural (rivers)—expansion brought on by "spurring," by the activity of unrestrained desire for dissolution in warfare. The result is not a human but an elemental context, a "gran tempesta" of excess even beyond the limits of ruin. Boiardo sees what Pulci saw, a stew or horrible mix, but Boiardo sees no good in it, no promise of vitalizing energy if one sups at this table. The inflamed souls, "gli animi di foco," finally become souls in flame, souls in hell.

Le lancie andarno in pezzi al cel volando,
Cadendo con romore al campo basso,
Scudo per scudo urtò, brando per brando,
Piastra per piastra insieme, a gran fraccasso.
Questa mistura a Dio la racomando:
Re, caval, cavalier sono in un fosso,
Cristiani e Saracini, e non discerno
Qual sia del celo, qual sia de l'inferno.

[II.xxx.47]

Lances go in pieces, flying toward the heavens,
Falling with noise to the plain below,
Shield screams on shield, sword on sword,
Armor plate on armor plate together, a great uproar;
This mixture I commend to God:
King, horse, knight are in a ditch,
Christians and Saracens, and I cannot tell
What is of heaven, what of hell.

What Pulci called a *mescuglio*, Boiardo calls a *mistura* ("mixture"); and as Pulci's term had its own echoes in the *Morgante* in *mortito* and *guazzabuglio*, so Boiardo's sets up its own peculiar resonances in the *Orlando Innamorato*. This is no *mortito* in a poem that loves ingestion, but a horrible *mistura* in a work that honors *misura*. It is significant that Boiardo says "a Dio la racomando," ("I commend [it] to God"), for he regards this awful mix of classes, races, and kinds as an affront to God's purpose and plan. Boiardo, always anxious to believe in a universe of proportion and hierarchy, is constantly disappointed.

He finally balances this grim *mistura* of kings, horses, and cavaliers at the end of Book II, with his own version of the benign and lovely mix a man can make later in Book III.

> Còlti ho diversi fiori alla verdura,
> Azuri, gialli, candidi e vermigli;
> Fatto ho di vaghe erbette una mistura,
> Garofili e vïole e rose e zigli:
> Traggasi avanti chi de odore ha cura,
> E ciò che più gli piace, quel se pigli;
> A cui diletta il ziglio, a cui la rosa,
> Ed a cui questa, a cui quella altra cosa.
>
> Però diversamente il mio verziero
> De Amore e de battaglie ho già piantato.
>
> [III.v. 1 – 2][17]

> I have gathered various flowers, of green,
> Blue, yellow, white, and vermilion;
> I have made from lovely plants a medley,
> Carnations and violets and roses and lilies:
> Let him come forward who cares for the scent,
> And whatever pleases, let him take;
> Whoever likes the lily, whoever the rose,
> And to him this, to him that other thing.
>
> Thus diversely my poetry
> Of Love and battle I have already planted.

Boiardo opposes the power of art to the energies of the battlefield. Here the *mistura* is a garden, where the diversity is of color and scent, under the control of the gardener-poet. The garden is an image of the poem, the poem an image of how things ought to be varied but orderly—like a garden. To say Boiardo retreats into art is an oversimplification, for art includes the potential for disaster, as the poem has. Rather, Boiardo retreats into images of the organic, or the natural, restrained. He chooses to emphasize the formal dimension of art, the impulse to control, rather than, with Pulci, to indulge the energy that lies under his hand. Boiardo is the poet of the curb rather than of the rider.

Boiardo's deepest desire is to conserve something of purpose in a world of confusion. He knows that chivalry is an outmoded system, but he wants to keep something of its value, its respect for grace and noble behavior, even while he relinquishes its forms and structures. Boiardo is trying, in short, to freeze the impulse to dissolve, the impulse that, with Pulci, he understands is instinctive to human life. Boiardo wants to check the urge to dissolution, to *sommergere,* that time seems inevitably to embody. He does not want to turn back the clock and regain the old world, but he does want to recapture the sense of control of oneself, if nothing else, that marked life under the old system. He wants to be able to praise something other than the giddy, headlong rush.

Boiardo makes his view of life explicit at the end of *Orlando Innamorato*. The last canto is only twenty-six stanzas long and is about the problems of control and the futility of desire in terms that we have come to regard as fundamental to the chivalric epic. Fiordespina is smitten with Bradamante, whom Fiordespina takes to be a male knight. To woo this knight, Fiordespina offers a gift, a splendid horse "forte e legiero" ("strong and nimble").

> un sol difetto avia,
> Che, potendo pigliar co' denti il morso,
> Al suo dispetto l'om portava via,
> Né si trovava a sua furia soccorso.
> Sol con parole si puotea tenire:
> Ciò sa la dama e ad altri non vol dire.
>
> [III.ix.8]

> One defect alone he had,
> That, taking the bit between his teeth,
> In his contempt he ran off with the man,
> Nor can he find help against [the horse's] fury;
> Only with a word can he be held in:
> The woman knows this [word] and doesn't want to tell [it to] others.

Here Boiardo reintroduces the image of the *cavallo sfrenato* and celebrates the power of language, or art, to control sheer, brute force. It is a word alone that can stop this runaway, a word that can freeze the rush to decay.

Bradamante mounts, the horse takes off, Fiordespina follows:

> E vede ben che la bocca ha sfrenata;
> Ora tira di possa, ora tira piano,
> Ma a ritenerlo ogni remedio è vano.
>
> [III.ix.19]

> And [Bradamante] sees well that the mouth is unchecked,
> Now pulls with strength, now pulls gently,
> But every effort to hold him in is vain.

Try as she might, Bradamante cannot "ritenne il cavallo sfrenato" ("hold in the unchecked horse," 20). One word will stop this mad dash toward a mountain covered by tangled growth—that is, this dash away from order and into the thicket of confusion. But few know the word, and those who do tend to forget what it is. Fiordespina suddenly cries out to the helpless rider:

> Non so come mi sia di mente uscito
> Di farti noto che il destrier, che ti ha
> Quasi condutto di morte al partito,
> Qualunche volta se gli dice: "Sta!"
> Non passarebbe più nel corso un dito;
> Ma, come io dissi, me dimenticai
> Farlo a te noto, e ciò mi dole assai.
>
> [III.ix.23]

> I don't know how it slipped my mind
> To tell you that the horse, who has

Almost taken you to your death at the outset,
Whenever you say to him "Stop!"
Wouldn't go any farther than a finger's length;
But, as I said, I forgot
To tell you, and I am very sorry.

Underneath what is funny and even ridiculous here, is a serious point. And that is once again we come back to love, the passion that leads one out of oneself; and, through love, we glimpse all the human passions that drive us out of control and send what we most value spinning toward death. The very obviousness of the words *Sta* or *Whoa* only serves to underscore the extremity of our need for something to stop the flight beyond *misura* to death, to stop the careening of history into chaos. And when in stanza 24 Bradamante finally cries "Sta!" to the horse of human impulse, the simple word works. The poet is able to envisage language as asserting control over matter, art as it can, in earnest or in game, regulate life. And yet while here we have an instance of what Boiardo always desires—the capacity of convention to curb sheer energy—the last stanza of the poem undercuts the victory man seems so narrowly to have won from time.

Mentre che io canto, o Iddio redentore,
Vedo la Italia tutta a fiama e a foco
Per questi Galli, che con gran valore
Vengon per disertar non so che loco;
Però vi lascio in questo vano amore
De Fiordespina ardente a poco a poco;
Un altra fïata, se mi fia concesso,
Racontarovi il tutto per espresso.

[III.ix.26]

While I sing, O my Redeemer,
I see Italy all in flames and fire,
Set by these Gauls, who with such valor
Come to ravage I don't know what place;
However, I leave you with this vain love
Of Fiordespina burning little by little;
Another time, if it's given me,
I'll tell you the rest explicitly.

That is all. And the "Sta!" that stops the poem, the word that reins in the glorious beast that is the *Orlando Innamorato*, is not the news of Charles VIII but, finally, the "vano amore." That is the final word, and vision—the fruitless desire of Fiordespina for Bradamante. Boiardo comes to see the futility of trying to control human desire; he sees the inability of the old way of life to check the human passions that must, after all, exist in order to animate life. There is no final staying of the steed save in poems, and poems—like the magic word—will often be forgotten and will always, finally, make very little difference.

At the end of the fourth canto of Book II, Boiardo has occasion to refer in passing to his art:

> Perché se dice che ogni bel cantare
> Sempre rincresce quando troppo dura,
> Ed lo diletto a tutti vi vo dare
> Tanto che basta, e non fuor di misura.
>
> [II.iv.86]

> Because it is said that every lovely song
> Always palls if it lasts too long
> And I want to give delight to everyone,
> In the proper amount, and not beyond measure.

Rincresce means not only "grows tiresome," but at its root means "grows weighty," "swells," "bloats." Even art is subject to its own laws of expansion; even language, for Boiardo the medium for establishing limitation, is subject to the urge to surpass limits. Art is not exempt from the very impulse it must control; the epic is finally an instance of the problem it describes. And the only recourse language has is to do what it says—is to fall silent after it has said "Stop!" The very meaning of his poem, that there is no way to check decay, in ourselves or our institutions, try as we might, dictated that Boiardo stop. There was no other way to end without reproducing chaos.

LUDOVICO ARIOSTO, *Orlando Furioso*[18]

In the fourth canto of *Orlando Furioso*, the putative hero, Ruggiero, is astride the splendid hippogriff: "Poggia l'augel, né può Ruggier frenarlo" ("The griffin soars, nor can Ruggiero [check it]," 49). The winged horse will not be curbed by the immature knight. The poem is, in many respects, about how Ruggiero grows up, how he grows into his role as founder of the Estensi, how he learns to check the forces outside and curb the energies within. This inability to refrain the hippogriff signals in Ruggiero a lack of vision, an imaginative weakness, an insufficiently developed perspective on the world. The winged horse, soaring over the earth, gives the broad, epic view of creation, and if one cannot control that medium for sight, one lacks insight in every sense. But what Ruggiero and so many others lack, Astolfo possesses in abundance. Astolfo is the master of perspective and control in this poem, and among other proofs of his privileged position we may note his handling of the same hippogriff.

> la sella sua, ch' appresso avea, gli messe;
> e gli fece, levando da più morsi
> una cosa et un' altra, un che lo resse;
> che dei destrier ch'in fuga erano corsi,
> quivi attaccate eran le briglie spesse.
>
> [XXII.28]

> [He placed] the saddle on him, which lay near, and
>   bitted
> The steed, by choosing, all the reins among,
> This part or that, until his mouth was fitted:
> For in that place were many bridles hung,
> Belonging to coursers which had flitted.

Like Pulci's Rinaldo at the scene of the horse fight, Ariosto's Astolfo offers us a version of the artist who disciplines the imagination by bridling the sheer energy it contains. As he chooses among the bits and bridles, Astolfo reflects the flexibility and shrewdness of the poet who must use not only what is at hand but also what is proper to the moment. Control of the winged horse figures control of one's intellective part, and that part of us, for Ariosto, is our destiny. For our intellect either accepts or transcends the codes and conventions, the social illusions, of life; it is the part that can destroy us or save us.

The image of the curbed or uncurbed horse occurs throughout the poem in a variety of ways. This is partly because there is in Ariosto a greater tendency than in Pulci or Boiardo to use the image for abstract purposes. We hear, for instance, about the curb of envy (XXVII.82), of shame (XXX.71), of courteous modesty (XLII.98); we hear of breaking the rein of shame (XXIX.30) or of patience (XXVIII.102); we hear of grief restrained (XLII.28). This tendency to exploit the metaphor in relation to abstract qualities or emotions is part of a larger intellectualizing impulse in the poem, a strain of abstract analysis that gives the poet's ironic scrutiny of human institutions such seeming distance and such power. This tendency toward abstraction also carries with it, and by no means always for ironic purposes, a moralizing streak, one that often emerges in the opening stanza of a given canto. For instance, Ruggiero rescues the naked Angelica:

> Quantunque debil freno a mezzo il corso
> animoso destrier spesso raccolga,
> raro è però che di ragione il morso
> libidinosa furia a dietro volga,
> quanto il piacere ha in pronto . . .
>
> [XI.1]

> Although a feeble rein, in mid-career,
> Will oft suffice to stop courageous horse:
> 'Tis seldom Reason's bit will serve to steer
> Desire, or turn him from his furious course,
> When pleasure is in reach.

Or later, when a beloved is threatened:

> Qual duro freno a qual ferrigno nodo,
> qual, s'esser può, catena di diamante
> farà che l'ira servi ordine e modo,
> che non trascorra oltre al prescritto inante,
> quando persona che con saldo chiodo
> t'abbia già fissa Amor nel cor costante,
> tu vegga o per violenzia o per inganno
> patire o disonore o mortal danno?
>
> [XLII.1]

What bit, what iron curb is to be found,
Or (could it be) what adamantine rein,
That can make wrath keep order and due bound,
And within lawful limits him contain?
When one, to whom the constant heart is bound,
And linked by Love with solid bolt and chain,
We see, through violence or through foul deceit,
With mortal damage or dishonor meet.

In both cases, the poet muses on the way powerful passions cannot be curbed by Reason's, or by a reasonable, rein; and in both cases, the sexual impulse, either as sheer lust in XI.1 or as Love, the spike *(chiodo)* in the heart, in XLII.1, goads the character, as both will goad Orlando, to excess. In XLII.1, Ariosto sees man as surpassing proper limit (l.4), much as Boiardo had invoked *misura* as his norm and Pulci had a sense of the game's limits, of the line the carpenter had to follow. Like his predecessors, Ariosto knows the urge to release will lead to shapelessness and decay. But he employs different terms.

Ariosto finally always sees *sfrenatura* as leading to fragmentation of the self, to the shattered or splintered personality—almost as if the self were a fragile artifact, susceptible to cracking under the pressure of convention and disillusionment. We get a glimpse of Ariosto's concept in XI.1, where he speaks of how a rein can the "animoso destrier spesso raccolga" ("[often gather in the lively beast]"). The idea of "gathering in" the horse, of integrating and consolidating the self, is at the heart of his vision. He is always concerned with the collected, as opposed to the dispersed or scattered, self.

Ariosto believes that to be collected or self-contained is the result of one's being flexible and adaptable; that one controls the self by serving no overmastering ideology, such as Chivalry or Petrarchan love or institutionalized religion. And he believes one is dispersed or "beside oneself" or, as he says, "di sé tolto," instead of "in sé raccolto," when one surrenders to the dictates of some social custom instead of acting as the time demands. Excess, or madness—and they are the same to this intensely practical but cerebral poet—occurs when we ignore our native *senno* ("[common] sense") for some system.

Ariosto is not cynical—Pulci is much more so—he is only conservative. They are very different attitudes.

Like Pulci and Boiardo, Ariosto conveys his version of restraint and release, or what I have called the collected and dispersed self, through the radical image of curbing the horse. In fact, the poet establishes this image and attitude at the outset of the poem. Angelica flees Rinaldo:

> La donna e il palafreno a dietro volta,
> e per la selva a tutta briglia il caccia;
> né per la rara più che per la folta,
> la più sicura e miglior via procaccia:
> ma pallida, tremando, e di sé tolta,
> lascia cura al destrier che la via caccia.
>
> [I.13]

> The affrighted damsel turns her palfrey round,
> And shakes the floating bridle in the wind;
> Nor in her panic seeks to choose her ground,
> Nor open grove prefers to thicket blind.
> But reckless, pale and trembling [and out of herself]
> Leaves to her horse the devious way to find.

The horse out of control is simply a symbol for human despair. When one is "beside oneself," *di sé tolto*, as Angelica is, one is *sfrenato* like the horse. How one rides is an index of one's spiritual state.

Orlando now becomes the focus of the poet's attention, in these terms, as Ariosto begins to point toward the middle of the poem and the core of the poem's meaning. Orlando is capable of acting in a rational, or collected, fashion, as Ariosto shows when Orlando rescues Olimpia from the ravenous orc: "Orlando in sé raccolto, / la mira altier, ne cangia cor ne volto" ("collected in himself, the peer / Looks proudly on, unchanged in heart and cheer," XI.35). Here he is integrated, not shattered, because his own passions and beliefs are not at issue; whereas, when he encounters his own needs, he goes, if you will, to pieces. For instance, after defeating Manilardo, Orlando pursues Angelica again:

Il suo camin (di lei chiedendo spesso)
or per li campi or per le selve tenne:
e sì come era uscito di sé stesso,
uscì dì strada.

[XII.86]

Through wood and field his courser did he goad,
Often inquiring for the royal dame:
Beside himself, he strayed beside the road.

Just as he is beside himself, so is he off the road. The dashing or
wandering horse is the fragmented self. As we know, Orlando is
capable of self-possession, of riding a straight line. But in the hostile
world of Romance (and Renaissance Italy), dispersal, the crooked
course, is the norm.

Canto XXIII is the middle canto of the completed poem and the
center of its meaning. All the energies and images of the *Orlando
Furioso* tend to flow into or out from this core. The cunning structure
of the canto would itself repay study, but suffice it to note here that
Bradamante's situation at the beginning of Canto XXIII accurately
catches up Orlando's predicament, in the terms we have been using,
and projects his massive agony to come. Bradamante wanders in the
night, searching for her beloved, Ruggiero:

Spesso di cor profondo ella sospira,
di pentimento e di dolor compunta,
ch'abbia in lei, più ch'amor, potuto l'ira.
—L'ira—dicea—m'ha dal mio amor disgiunto.

[XXIII.7]

With sorrow and repentance oft assailed,
She from her inmost heart profoundly sighed,
That Anger over Love should have prevailed.
["Anger," she said, "has displaced me from my love."]

Here the sinister echo in line 3 of Dante's Ugolino ("Poscia, più che 'l
dolor, poté 'l digiuno"—"Till hunger over grief at last prevailed,"
Inferno XXXIII.75) startles us and deepens our sense of disjunction,
of the way that madness, because of love, will only separate us farther

from those we love, and from ourselves. Here is all the rhetoric of the shattered self in half an octave.

Ariosto now brings Orlando to the fore, and shrewdly reintroduces the crucial image of the horse and curb. Orlando fights mighty Mandricardo:

> Sta in sé raccolto Orlando, e ne va verso
> il suo vantaggio, e alla vittoria aspira:
> gli pon la cauta man sopra le ciglia
> del cavallo, e cader ne fa la briglia.
>
> [XXIII.86]

> Firm in his stirrups self-collected stood
> Roland, and watched his vantage to obtain;
> He to the other courser's forehead slipt
> His wary hand, and thence the bridle stript.

As in the battle with the orc (XI.35), Orlando is self-possessed when confronted by an external force or foe. Ariosto implies again, as he does so often, that we are only really fragmented in our dealings with ourselves. Now the bridle is off Mandricardo's horse, as Orlando at least symbolically unleashes the forces of ruin, the energies of self-destruction. Orlando falls; Mandricardo's horse—"Il destrier c'ha la testa in libertade, / quello a chi tolto era il freno di bocca" ("[The horse whose head is free, / who had the bit removed from his mouth]," 88)—dashes off. By emphasizing the horse's *sfrenato* condition, Ariosto sets up an ironic contrast between the man who was sufficiently "in sé raccolto" to release the curb, and the horse from whom "tolto il freno era di bocca." The rest of the canto describes how the man loses himself and becomes the horse.

Mandricardo's runaway mount finally hurtles into a ditch: "Quivi si ferma il corridore al fine; / ma non si può guidar, che non ha freno" ("Here stopt the horse; but him he could not guide, / Left without bit his motions to restrain," 91). There can be no advancement without restraint—a basic paradox in the poem, and in all these Renaissance poems. But in the same octave Doralice offers her bridle to Mandricardo, who refuses (92), but who snatches the bridle from the approaching Gabrina, whose horse then runs madly away (93–94). What Ariosto leaves us with is the image of curbing and releasing violently expanded, of life as an endless chain of runaways, as potentially always out of control. All of this is preparing for Orlando's final agony.

Orlando now follows the strange course of Mandricardo's mount for two days, until he comes to a lovely garden clearing, which in many ways reminds us of Alcina's isle-garden and of Ruggiero's arrival there (VI.20–24). The reminiscence is appropriate, for in its way this place will be as different from what it appears to be as that one was. Here the pastoral spot will be the seat of madness, as Ariosto begins to concentrate his attack on those traditions and conventions that take us out of ourselves, that give us assumptions about life and the world that are false, and that the world does not or cannot sustain.

As he looks around, Orlando sees *scritti* (102; 106), *lettere* (103), *parole* (106)—all the trees have inscriptions carved into them telling of the passionate love between Medoro and Angelica. This is an assault on the convention of Petrarchan love on two levels. First, Orlando's (ultimately) *fin amors* and Petrarchan ideas about the aspiring lover and the disdainful lady are shattered because the lady is supposed to reject all amorous approaches, and here, as the inscriptions make very clear, Angelica has succumbed. Orlando's assumptions about the conventions of love and courtship are thus destroyed. But Ariosto also attacks the love that is consummated, showing it not to be a tender, if realistic, romance between the princess and the soldier, but rather, beneath the elegant language of love, a crude transaction in physical needs. For instance, stanza 108, one of the inscriptions, opens with clear Petrarchan echoes: "Liete piante, verdi erbe, limpide acque" (["Smiling plants, green meadows, clear waters"]) but at the end it says of Angelica:

> "spesso ne le mie braccia nuda giacque;
> de la commodità che qui m'è data,
> io povero Medoro ricompensarvi
> d'altro non posso, che d'ognior lodarvi."

> ["Often in my arms she naked lay;
> For the commodity that is here given me,
> I poor Medoro cannot recompense you
> Except to sing your every praise."]

The description of Angelica naked does not destroy our illusions; it is the attitude toward her, the language of the marketplace—*commodity, poor, recompense*—that makes the girl meat and shows praise of her to be the only coin in which he can pay her. Ariosto is attacking the social myths and their conventional language because they lie.

Indeed, lying is a fundamental point to this lovely wood of words out of which madness comes. We feel more and more the presence of language on the trees, until the wood is a forest of verbal signs and Orlando is trapped in it, unable to believe their significance but forced to believe it, in either case the victim of the *scritti*. This is the dilemma Ariosto sees all of us confronted with; as readers of the poem, we are faced, as Orlando is, with words that are deceptive, inherently deceitful, the medium for fictions, but words that also tell us a hard truth. And that truth is that as people in the real world, we are faced (like Orlando in the poem) with symbols, codes, and conventions that may not simply shatter us but may also give our lives meaning and coherence. In short, Orlando in the wood of words is Ariosto's image for the reader in the poem, for the reader in the world, and for the tragic predicament he faces: unwilling to believe what he must believe in, and, when forced to believe, shattered as a result.

Orlando gathers himself to lie to himself:

> Poi ritorna in sé alquanto, e pensa come
> possa esser che non sia la cosa vera.
>
> [XXIII. 144]
>
> He somewhat [gathered himself in], and thought
> How possibly the thing might not be true.

But it avails nothing. After spending a night in the same cabin they stayed in, hemmed in by even more inscriptions, trapped in the reality of their fiction, Orlando is told by a shepherd the *istoria* of

Medoro and Angelica.[19] And then, in a literalization of the hard truth, Orlando is shown the gem Angelica gave the shepherd when they left.

> Questa conclusion ful la secure
> che 'l capo a un colpo gli levò dal collo.
>
> [XXIII.121]

> A deadly axe was this unhappy close,
> Which, at a single stroke, lopt off his head.

Orlando is truly beside himself; what happened to the horses of Mandricardo and Gabrina—loss of control of the head—has happened to him. Ariosto then signals the release of grief (and madness) with the image we have been observing: "Poi ch'allargare il freno al dolor puote / (che resta solo e senza altrui rispetto)" ("[Then] he can give the rein to raging woe, / Alone, by other's presence unreprest," 122). He is the horse, unrestrained, something mad in his energy and not human. His radical dislocation is communicated by his headlessness, his condition that of a "cavallo sfrenato."

Then follows the great statement in the poem of the dispersed or divided self. Orlando cries out:

> Non son, non sono io quel che paio in viso:
> quel ch'era Orlando è morto et è sotterra;
> la sua donna ingratissima l'ha ucciso:
> sì, mancando di fé, gli ha fatto guerra.
> Io son lo spirito suo da lui diviso,
> ch'in questo inferno tormentandosi erra,
> acciò con l'ombra sia, che sola avanza,
> esempio a chi in Amor pone speranza.
>
> [XXIII.128]

> I am not—am not what I seem in sight:
> What Roland was is dead and under ground,
> Slain by that most ungrateful lady's spite,
> Whose faithlessness inflicted such a wound.
> Divided from the flesh, I am his sprite,
> Which in this hell, tormented, walks its round,

> To be, but in its shadow left above,
> A warning to all such as trust in love.

Now Orlando is not simply a victim of the fact things are not what they seem; he embodies that fact. Illusion is the essence of existence. And the result of this situation, and knowledge, is that man is radically divided against, and within, himself. Here is Ariosto's greatest appeal for prudence and self-possession and for a willingness to live within limitation, and his greatest warning against putting one's faith and hope in any system, verbal or cultural. For the end of such wholesome faith will only be despair and division.

Orlando is mad. And his madness grows, "Che fuor del senno al fin l'ebbe condotto" (["Until it had led far beyond good sense"], 137). Ariosto, typically, introduces that quality he values most, *senno*, good or common sense, by telling us it has been lost. In stanza 133, the essential, brute man emerges when Orlando strips off his armor, thus shedding chivalry, for once he is bereft of his reason, he must jettison the civilized trappings that symbolized, and also undermined, reason. Now Orlando is defined by his real needs, not by social norms, and like any of the runaway horses we have seen, he plunges on into the woods. The terrible weight of conventional assumptions has shattered this man, as, according to the poet, it will shatter any one of us. Like his predecessors, Ariosto has used the spectacle of the horse and the metaphor of curbing to show us the loss of control that invariably results from substituting something else for one's native *senno*.

The story of Orlando is resumed in Canto XXIX, where many of these insights are clarified and extended. Orlando sees Angelica and Medoro and gives chase. She uses her magic ring to disappear and Orlando seizes her mare "ch'un altro avrebbe fatto una donzella" (["as another would have seized a girl,"] 68). Here the identification between sexual activity and riding, hinted at humorously elsewhere (VIII.49–50, XXVIII.64), is made serious and explicit, and the mad fury of Orlando is given a powerful sexual source and meaning. As he rides her horse into the ground and kills it, it is clear that he has released on the mare the sexual energy that, according to social and "poetic" custom, he had to restrain with her mistress. And after the horse dies and he simply drags her over the ground, "Orlando non le pensa e non la guarda, / e via correndo il suo camin non tarda" ("Orlando nought the slaughtered mare regards, / Nor anywise his headlong course retards," 71). He has truly become the "cavallo sfrenato" once more, his human sexual fury spent, his bestial nature now unchecked. In Canto XXX, he finally rides another horse straight into the sea (12–14), as Ariosto exploits the imagery of dissolution and submersion we saw in Pulci and Boiardo, the fatal tendency in man to succumb to the rush of instinct and to lose all human shape. But the most powerful image is that of the huge, naked man dragging the dead mare. This is Ariosto's most arresting vision of man's sexual need spurring him beyond reason, and of chivalry as a burden, a dead weight to be borne even when it is without life or significance.

The *senno* Orlando lost at XXIII.132 is recovered by Astolfo at XXXIV.66, on the moon.[20] Astolfo brings Orlando's *senno* back to earth to where the mighty madman is bound fast. Orlando inhales from the proffered vial and sanity returns. Then Orlando, restored, wonders at his bound condition:

> Poi disse, come già disse Sileno
> a quei che lo legàr nel cavo speco:
> *Solvite me*, con viso sì sereno,
> con guardo sì men de l'usato bieco,
> che fu slegato.
>
> [XXXIX.60]

> Then said, as erst Silenus said—when seen,
> And taken sleeping in the cave of yore—
> SOLVITE ME, with visage so serene,
> With look so much less wayward than before,
> That him they from his bonds delivered clean.

Orlando echoes Virgil's Silenus (*Eclogue* VI.24: "Solvite me, pueri: satis est potuisse videri" ["Loose me, lads; enough that you have shown your power"]), a bucolic reminiscence that cures the madness acquired in a pastoral place. As we said before, our tragic predicament is that tradition and convention can sustain us as well as destroy us, cure as well as kill. There are no easy answers.

Now the great cry for release expands on all the former images of restraint, as Orlando has finally learned that external curbs are unnecessary if a man checks his internal energies himself. He who was like, and then was, a "cavallo sfrenato" can now be a Silenus freed, because he knows the only true and effective check is his own *senno*, his own sense of limit and inner government matched to the moment. As the former images of unrefrained energy find their proper answer in this example of the man who checks himself, so *senno* restored brings with it the "viso . . . sereno." Throughout the poem, *senno* is finally opposed to *sfrenatura, serenità* to the person *di sé tolto*.[21]

At the end of the *Orlando Furioso*, all we have learned through Orlando's plight in Canto XXIII, and what went into and came out of that canto, is manifest in history. Ruggiero and Bradamante will found the Este line. But at their marriage, the forces of disunity, in Rodomonte, intrude to shatter the new integration of might and grace, Saracen convert and native Christian, male and female (XLVI.101f.). Ruggiero and Rodomonte then engage in a titanic struggle before the wedding guests, in a way dispersing the energy already so carefully gathered and woven—as in the poem—into the wedding tent and nuptial bed (XLVI.77f.). Rodomonte seizes Ruggiero by the throat and throws him to the ground. At this critical moment, when everything that was gathered in threatens to become dispersed, Ruggiero looks at his bride: "e turbar vide il bel viso sereno" ("[And troubled sees] that fair face serene," 125). The vision of secular serenity, the most we can hope for here below, inspires Ruggiero, and he reasserts himself. The battle is tremendous, but finally

> Ruggier sta in sé raccolto, e metter in opra
> senno e valor, per rimaner di sopra.
>
> [133]
>
> Collected in himself, Ruggiero wrought
> [Sense and courage, to remain on top.]

What we can have—not what we ought to have—energizes Ruggiero to collect himself and to rely on what is best within him, and not on what society prescribes for him. Angelica, "di sé tolto" by love in Canto I, is matched by Ruggiero, "in sé raccolto" for love in Canto XLVI.

The ironies of this final resolution, of course, are clear, for much as Ruggiero is able to restrain, or gather and thus effectively release all his *virtù*, our last view is of the bridegroom embracing not the bride but his male enemy, not new life but death. Our final view is of how, at the beginning of Este history, only the past was reenacted when the future was meant to be projected, how war was the constant norm where peace was supposed to rule. Like Virgil, whose epic's last line his last line echoes, Ariosto sees hope as streaked by melancholy and futility, the civic order as always prey to the individual's impulse to decay. But this resolution—momentary, tenuous—and the story of Orlando, who learned how a man becomes headless and runs away, beside himself, into the forests of despair, and how he can come back, is the paradigm for man's excesses and for the self-imposed limitations that will be his salvation.

Later the chivalric epic would change. In Tasso, the impulse to dispersal and the need for limit would become part of the very structure of his epic as well as themes in it. In Spenser's *Faerie Queene* and Cervantes's *Don Quixote*, the necessity to refrain our instinct to transform would produce great, elegiac epic visions. But the radical issues are established in Pulci, Boiardo, and Ariosto, in those poets who understood first the limits of the world they so loved, who knew that we swell toward death in pursuit of what is most vital in us, who knew that artistic creation is, finally, a version of the problem of restraint and release that the work of art describes. These were the poets who understood how deep into our common humanity the simple image and act of restraining a horse could go.

4

Spenser: From Magic to Miracle

"We are on enchanted ground, my friend," says Bishop Hurd of Romance in the sixth of his *Letters on Chivalry and Romance*: a world, he says later of the Italian poets, where "anything is enough to be the basis for their air-form'd visions" (Letter X). But, if Hurd recognizes the visionary part of Romance, he also knows that reason is gaining ascendancy "over the portentous spectres of the imagination. . . . So that Milton, as fond as we have seen he was of the Gothic fictions, durst only admit them of the bye, and in the way of simile and illustration only." "Instead of Giants and Magicians," says Hurd of Milton, "he had Angels and Devils to supply him with the *marvelous*, with greater probability" (Letter XII).[1]

I want to survey that "enchanted ground" from a particular vantage point. My perspective on the chivalric romances of Spenser and his Italian predecessors will be on perspective in those poems, on one of the ways the poems deal with the problem of seeing and the necessities for sight. Though not in the manner of Bishop Hurd, I will be concerned with Romance's visionary part, with how and what one sees when standing on enchanted ground. And my argument will be that throughout the tradition of chivalric romance one is offered moments of divine vision or revelation, visions connected with the simple gesture of raising a visor or a helmet. Thus, when a poet like Milton, in Hurd's language, substitutes the Christian marvelous for

Gothic enchantment, we are not witnessing a radical break with the past so much as the completion of an impulse implicit in chivalric romance all along.

This impulse to reveal divinity is manifest when a visor or helmet is raised.[2] At that moment the reader, or protagonist, of chivalric romance—or both—discovers an image of permanence and perfection through the reconciliation of opposites. These versions of stability, of certainty, are so crucial because they are what Romance, at its heart, constantly yearns for.

The world of Romance is always seen as in flux and of flux, a world where change, reversal, and discovery work through Time, Time whose power, we are reminded in *The Winter's Tale*, is

> To o'erthrow law, and in one self-born hour
> To plant and o'erwhelm custom.
>
> [IV.i.8–9]

It is a world where the enchanted ground is always shifting. Within this flux lies Romance's visionary core, whose burning integrity, if only we can perceive it, can redeem the ravages of mortality. When in chivalric romance the moment of vision or revelation occurs, we are summoned from shimmering vistas of magic to stable peaks of miracle. We are delivered, if only briefly, from the sway of Ovid to the certainties of Virgil. Ovid is the patron saint of Romance mutability, Virgil the father of its visionary core. The narrative modes of Romance are all implicit in Daphne's flight from Apollo, while Romance's visionary impulse, its radical hunger for certainty and divinity, is incarnate in Venus, revealed as a goddess to her errant, baffled son. Ovid stands behind the Angelicas and Florimells fleeing their tormentors; Virgil behind Hermione stepping down to Perdita.

Before surveying the momentary transformations of magic into miracle in *The Faerie Queene*, we will glance at some Italian poets. My apology for the necessarily allusive nature of this essay is that, with Astolfo, I have found the only way to cover enchanted ground is by hippogriff.

In canto **XXXII** of Ariosto's *Orlando Furioso*,[3] Bradamante reveals herself. First there is jesting about the shining hair of Britomart's great precursor:

> La donna cominciando a disarmarsi
> L'avea lo scudo e dipoi l'elmo tratto;
> Quando una cuffia d'oro, in che celarsi
> Soleano i capei lunghi e star di piatto,
> Uscí con l'elmo; onde caderon sparsi
> Giù per le spalle, e la scopriro a un tratto
> E la feron conoscer per donzella,
> Non men che fiero in arme, in viso bella.
>
> [XXXII.79]

> The woman began to disarm herself;
> First her shield, then her helmet she took off;
> When a golden hairnet, in which her long hair
> Usually hid itself and stayed in place,
> Fell with the helmet; whence the hair fell
> Down to her shoulders and revealed her suddenly
> And made her known as a maiden,
> No less beautiful of face than fierce in arms.

As is often the case with this motif, the revelation is communicated in terms of opposites reconciled, here a masculine might and a feminine beauty contained and displayed in the single figure of Bradamante. Ariosto, however, further refines our perception of this revelation in the next octave.

> Quale a cader de le cortine suole
> Parer fra mille lampade la scena,
> D'archi, e di più una superba mole,
> D'oro, e di statue, e di pittura piena;
> O come suol fuor de le nube il sole
> Scoprir la faccia limpida e serena,
> Così l'elmo levandosi dal viso
> Mostrò la donna aprisse il paradiso.
>
> [XXXII.80]

As when a theater curtain customarily falls aside,
The scene appears amidst a thousand lamps,
Full of arches, and then a splendid hill,
And statues of gold and pictures;
Or when the sun is accustomed through clouds
To discover its face glistening and serene;
So the helmet, raised from the face,
Showed the woman, opened paradise.

The simile of the theater curtain, from Ovid (*Met.* III.111–14), communicates the sudden, brilliant completeness of the revelation, while the simile of the sun, shining clear and serene through clouds, shifts our gaze, again through glistening light, to the heavens. The last couplet completes the analogy and then, as the syntax collapses, identifies Bradamante with paradise. The maiden herself is now an image of that happy place.[4]

These paradoxes reconciling opposites, the images of light, the promise of paradise, are the common terms of Boiardo, Ariosto's master in the world of chivalric romance. Near the end of his massive *Orlando Innamorato* (III.v.38), Boiardo says that Bradamante wanted to see Ruggiero's visor-covered face more than she wanted to see paradise itself.[5] And when three octaves later she reveals her face to him through an upraised visor, we hear of her golden hair, but more of her face, where "a certain delicacy / Was mixed with vigor and strong desire" ("una delicatezza / Mescolata di ardire e di vigore," 41). Her "angelic face" (42) combines divinity and humanity, strength and tenderness, male and female, in a vision so perfect, Boiardo says, he cannot even describe it (41).

Ariosto and Boiardo present us with a Camilla who then reveals herself as a kind of Beatrice. Indeed it is to Dante's Beatrice we must turn, for from her revelation to the pilgrim in Eden the Italian poets, and thence others, derive their language of vision and their image of a woman who embodies bliss beyond the reach of change.

In *Purgatory* XXX,[6] preceded by the words which presaged Christ, Beatrice is revealed to her trembling lover:

> Io vidi già nel cominciar del giorno
> la parte orïental tutta rosata,
> e l'altro ciel di bel sereno adorno;
> e la faccia del sol nascere ombrata,
> sì che, per temperanza di vapori,
> l'occhio la sostenea lunga fiata:
> cosi dentro una nuvola di fiori
> che dalle mani angeliche saliva
> e ricadeva in giù dentro e di fori,
> sovra candido vel cinta d'uliva
> donna m'apparve, sotto verde manto
> vestita di color di fiamma viva

[ll. 22–33]

> I once saw at the beginning of the day,
> the eastern part of the sky all rosy
> and the rest clear and beautiful;
> And the face of the sun came forth shaded
> so that through the tempering vapours
> the eye could bear it long;
> So within a cloud of flowers,
> which rose from the angel's hands
> and fell again within and without,
> A lady appeared to me, bound with olive
> over a white veil, clothed under a green mantle
> with the color of flame.

Only later will Dante see directly: now he looks through veils, as if seeing the sun through clouds. But the language and, I would argue, the significance of the profound revelation are adapted by the poets of chivalric romance for their visions discovered through a raised visor or discarded helmet. No Beatrice is Bradamante; but her magic armor can still reveal miracle.

In the third canto of his *Morgante*, the first of the great Italian writers of Romance, Luigi Pulci,[7] tells us how the ubiquitous Orlando wounds a knight; it is the girl Meridïana.

> l'elmo gli uscì, la treccia si vedea,
> che raggia come stelle per sereno,

anzi pareva di Venere iddea,
anzi quella che è fatta un alloro,
anzi parea d'argento, anzi pur d'oro.

[III.17]

the helmet falls, he sees the hair
which shines like stars in the heavens;
in fact, she looks like the goddess Venus;
in fact, like the girl who was made a laurel;
in fact, like silver; in fact, like gold.

Pulci, whose facial expression is always something between a sneer and a tired smile, discovers for us the classical roots of this tradition of revelation. Not in the figure of Daphne, here because in *Metamorphoses* I her golden hair is emphasized on three occasions (477, 497, 542), but in Venus and in the gold and silver. For behind Pulci, and all the poets we have noted, are the revelations of Venus to Aeneas and of Aeneas to Dido in Book I of the *Aeneid*.[8] First the goddess:

Dixit et avertens rosea cervice refulsit,
ambrosiaeque comae divinum vertice odorem
spiravere; pedes vestis defluxit ad imos,
et vera incessu patuit dea.

[ll.402–05]

She spoke, and as she turned her rosy neck flashed
and from her head ambrosial hair breathed divine fragrance,
her garment fell around her feet,
and where she walked she was revealed, a true goddess.

Later, her godlike son steps from his surrounding cloud:

restitit Aeneas claraque in luce refulsit,
os umerosque deo similis; namque ipsa decoram
caesariem nato genetrix lumenque iuventae
purpureum et laetos oculis adflarat honores;
quale manus addunt ebori decus, aut ubi flavo
argentum Pariusve lapis circumdatur auro.

[ll.588–93]

Aeneas stood forth, and gleamed bright in the clear light,
in shape and face like a god; his mother had given

him the beauty of flowing hair, and youth's ripe bloom,
And in his eyes a joyous light—like the sheen the hand
gives ivory, or when silver or Parian marble is set in gold.

Both Virgilian passages, emphasizing revelations through veils or
clouds of shining faces and hair, underscore divinity, and derive from
the moment Venus first appears, disguised, to Aeneas:

o—quam te memorem, virgo? namque haud tibi voltus
mortalis, nec vox hominem sonat; o dea certe!

[I.327–28]

But what shall I call you, o maiden?—neither your
face is mortal, nor has your voice a human ring;
O surely a goddess!

O dea certe: the chivalric romance will dis-cover goddesses through
cloudy veils, and visors, and each revelation will offer an instance of
miraculous stability in a world of ceaseless change.[9] My aim, however, is not to track the spoor of sources, nor hermetically to seal
"influences"; I want simply to identify an impulse animating chivalric romance in the Renaissance so as better to approach some motifs
Spenser uses, for his own particular purposes, in *The Faerie Queene*.

   Moments of vision or revelation are much more frequent, and
dense, in *The Faerie Queene* than in any preceding Romance; we are
constantly offered such moments, from the primary level of visors
raised and veils laid aside, to the grand visions in the tenth cantos of
Books I, IV, and VI or the dream at Isis Church in V.vii. These
moments recur so frequently because in this world of corrosive
mutability, they are at once so evanescent and yet so necessary
and desired. The poet constantly returns to these moments because
Spenser's whole impulse is to flesh out the ideal, to grapple, or moor,
the visionary to the real world; he is forever seeking a language, a
grammar, that will be sufficiently suggestive and rare, even in-
cantatory, and yet supple and generously mundane enough to capture
and hold these moments of revelation intact. Where the Italian poets
tended to concentrate on the effect of the vision or revelation on the

beholder,[10] Spenser, with crucial and obvious exceptions, usually fastens on the quality of the vision itself.

By holding these moments aloft, as it were, Spenser hopes to discover permanence behind change and thus shape the perspective of his reader. The poet's goal is to teach us to distinguish between magic and miracle, between what is only vain appearance and a moment of divinity. He wants to reform our sight from that of *voyeurs* to that of *voyants*, from the gaze of spies to the vision of seers, always teaching us to see at once beneath and beyond what appears.

I can do no more than sketch the way these moments of divinity work in *The Faerie Queene*. In Book I, canto iii, our single gesture reveals two very different perspectives. At stanza 38, Sansloy overcomes a knight:

> rudely rending vp his helmet, [he] would
> Haue slaine him straight; but when he sees his age,
> And hoarie head of *Archimago* old,
> His hastie hand he doth amazed hold.

Contrasted with this revelation of falsity incarnate is the vision of truth some thirty stanzas earlier, when Una, "farre from all mens sight,"

> From her faire head her fillet she vndight,
> And laid her stole aside. Her angels face
> As the great eye of heauen shyned bright,
> And made a sunshine in the shadie place;
> Did neuer mortall eye behold such heauenly grace.
>
> [I.iii.4]

By contrasting the revelations of Archimago to Sansloy and of Una to the reader, Spenser is educating us to the fact that not all revelations are the same; not all are benign.[11] In this poem, a single gesture or impulse or activity can lead in completely opposite directions: context is all, wherein we must exercise our wary judgment. For instance, compare the two dream visions of beloved women in Book I: Red Cross's in I.i.47−50, Arthur's in I.ix.13−15. Because Red Cross believes what he sees, he earns Duessa and eventually despair;

whereas Arthur, after his dream of the Faery Queene, offers us an image of the whole poem's effort to incarnate an ideal:

> From that day forth I lou'd that face diuine;
> From that day forth I cast in carfull mind,
> To seek her out with labour and long tyne,
> And neuer vow to rest, till her I fynd.
>
> [I.ix.15]

Arthur's effort to make the divine face human; the poet's effort to grapple vision to the world with words, is parodied in Book II when Braggadocchio attempts to ravish Belphoebe (II.iii.42) and is re-affirmed when Arthur notes the Faery Queene's "full lively" image on Guyon's shield in canto ix, stanza 3.[12]

Books I and II introduce us, then, to the difficult process of distinguishing kinds of magic from shapes of miracle, and of making miracle permanent in mutable human affairs; Books III, IV, and V embody this process, and thus parallel the quest of Arthur, in the figures of Britomart and Artegall. As was Bradamante in the Italian romances, Britomart will be the conduit for much of the poem's visionary energy. In her, as Spenser says at III.i.46, "aimiable grace, / and manly terrour mixed therewithall,"[13] and at Malbecco's, at canto ix, after "vailed was her loftie crest" (20), the guests are fixed

> In contemplation of diuinitie:
> But most they maruailed at her cheualree
> and noble prowesse.
>
> [III.ix.24]

Reconciling the opposites of male strength and feminine grace, at once an object of contemplation and a model of active power, she embodies a Renaissance version of perfection. But it is Britomart's face, blazing through her visor, that reveals her divinity throughout, and the language of the description at III.i.42−43 not only recalls the images of the Italian poets but also anticipates the language of the visions through her visor used at III.ix.20, IV.i.13, and IV.vi.22.

> [She] vented vp her vmbriere,
> And so did let her goodly visage to appere.
> As when faire *Cynthia*, in darksome night,
> Is in a noyous cloud enueloped,
> Where she may find the substaunce thin and light,
> Breakes forth her siluer beames, and her bright hed
> Discouers to the world discomfited;
> Of the poore traueller, that went astray,
> With thousand blessing she is heried;
> Such was the beautie and the shining ray,
> With which faire *Britomart* gaue light vnto the day.
>
> [III.i.42–43]

The image of her face, shining as does the moon through clouds, participates in more than a tradition of romance imagery. These lines, promising steadfastness in terms of guidance to weary travelers, recall all those images in *The Faerie Queen* and the *Epithalamium* of fixed stars guiding wanderers and of lodestars hidden behind clouds—images of beneficent or lost fixity, unconnected to visors or veils, which seem to come from the poet's deepest being.[14]

While Britomart appears perfect and steadfast, she seeks, like Arthur, to realize a vision of love. For she saw in her father's "mirrhour fayre"

> A comely knight, all arm'd in complete wize,
> Through whose bright ventayle, lifted vp on hye,
> His manly face, that did his foes agrize,
> And friends to termes of gentle truce entize,
> Lookt forth . . .
>
> [III.ii.24]

It is Artegall's face, like Phoebus out of the East.

Thus in the first two cantos of Book III, we have two revelations through visors: one of Britomart and one to Britomart. She must now match her face to his, and in tempering Artegall's power with her chaste, affectionate grace effect a perfect union. The process of accommodating ideal opposites to human form is a long one and never permanently accomplished in this world of change for this pair any more than any other. But there is a moment in Book IV when vision is made flesh, when what we want and what we can have fleetingly meet. In canto vi of Book IV, Artegall unknowingly smites Britomart:

> Her ventayle shard away. . . .
> With that her angels face, vnseen afore,
> Like to the ruddie morne appeard in sight,
> Deawed with siluer drops, through sweating sore.
>
> [19]

The divine face is made human by the sweat, those silver drops which in themselves reconcile the orders of art and nature. And when he sees this face at once angelic and earthly, Artegall

> At last fell humbly downe vpon his knee,
> And of his wonder made religion.
>
> [22]

Wonder made religion—here magic is made miracle; this is the heart of Romance as by Revelation we apprehend divinity and comprehend steadfastness out of flux and shadowy ignorance.

There will be other discoveries in the poem: most notably Artegall, at V.v.12 – 13, will see Radigund through a visor as he saw Britomart and will succumb to pity, where once, he knelt before a kind of grace.[15] And visions will abound in Book VI, not those through a visor, but visions of a wider, more communal kind as befits Courtesy—visions of women ringed in harmony: Elizabeth by courtiers in the Proem (st. 7), Serena ringed by savages at canto viii.39; Pastorella by shepherds in canto ix.8, and the girl ringed by graces and maidens on Mount Acidale in canto x.12. Indeed, the shepherds around Pastorella who "oft for wonder shout,"

> As if some miracle of heauenly hew
> Were downe to them descended in that earthly vew
>
> [VI.ix.8]

have made their wonder, religion. They have seen miracle incarnate on the enchanted ground, and in their "shouts" of joy the maker of

Colin Clout may have both concealed his deepest hopes and revealed his despair at finding a language to express what they saw.[16]

The visor that conceals and reveals divinity is simply a chivalric variant on the Silenus Alcibiades, that statuette mentioned by Plato (*Symposium*, 215) whose crude exterior hid the luminous god. This figure, like the image of the husk and the kernel, was a favorite Renaissance emblem for poetry, and whole poems.[17] In this sense, *The Faerie Queene* is a Silenus, for Spenser—exploiting the language of veils and vision—directs us to lovely truth hidden in his poem.

> Vnfitly I these ydle rimes present,
> The labor of lost time, and wit vnstayd:
> Yet if their deeper sence be inly wayd,
>   And the dim vele, with which from comune vew
>   Their fairer parts are hid, aside be layd.
> Perhaps not vaine they may appeare to you.
>   [Commendatory sonnet to Lord Burleigh]

To sum up the significance of the visor and of vision and revelation in the romances of Spenser and his Italian predecessors, we can do no better than cite the poet who knew them best and surpassed them. At the beginning of Book III of *Paradise Lost*, Milton says:

>   Thus with the year
> Seasons return, but not to me returns
> Day, or the sweet approach of Ev'n or Morn,
> Or sight of vernal bloom, or Summer's Rose,
> Or flocks, or herds, or human face divine;
> But cloud instead, and ever-during dark
> Surrounds me . . .
> So much the rather thou Celestial Light
> Shine inward, and the mind through all her powers
> Irradiate, there plant eyes, all mist from thence
> Purge and disperse, that I may see and tell
> Of things invisible to mortal sight.
>   [40–46, 51–55]

In the raising of a visor, and all it means, we may see things invisible to mortal sight in revelations of the human face divine shining through, purging and dispersing, the clouds. For Spenser the discovery of that divine face made human represents the evanescent moment to which he constantly returns, as he tries to seize the moment through language and thus reform the deformations wrought by Time and chance and change. Like Prince Arthur, his Roland, his Aeneas, Spenser strives to find a way to make the vision real; for, like his hero, Spenser wants to raise the final visor, lay aside the final dim veil, finally discover the face he worshiped most, the true and abiding face of his Queen, and of her green and pleasant land.

5

Primitivism and the Process of Civility in Spenser's Faerie Queene

The Other World of folklore had suddenly become the New World of fact. The medieval locale of enchantment and perfect satisfaction found itself realized, so it seemed, in the Novus Mundus of Columbus. While the Spanish would call the new place "otro mundo" or Indies long after other names had been found, the English begin referring to it as *America* as early as 1519.[1] However, something of the older sense of medieval dreams underlying Renaissance realities still occurs in England in 1651 when, in a derisive medical treatise, Noah Biggs can refer to "the *New-found-Land* of *Americall* or *Prestor-John* humours."[2] I will look at precisely this mix of attitudes, this engagement of something new-found that recalls older dreams, in *The Faerie Queene*. Through Spenser's poem I want to suggest some approaches to the question of what the Renaissance did with new-found things, and how in the process of shaping the new in the image of the old, the very nature of recreation and renaissance is explored.[3]

Spenser is aware of the "other world" as well as the "new world." He incorporates the Spanish view by referring twice to "Indian Peru" (II.proem.2; III.iii.6) and to various savages or savage impulses, like Maleger or Fansy in Cupid's Masque, as Indians (II.xi.21–22; III.xii.8)—Indians that have to be tamed. But the man who wrote the letter to Raleigh also knew about "fruitfullest Virginia" (II.proem.2), named for the Virgin Queene in 1587, and he knew the name America. Mercilla, another version of Elizabeth, is said to have "enlarged" her rule

> From th' utmost brinke of the Americke shore
> Unto the margent of the Molucas.
>
> [V.x.3][4]

Earlier, in Book II, in the *Antiquitee of Faery Lond* that Guyon read at the top of Alma's Castle, we had heard how the first offspring of Elfe and Fay, Elfin, had first ruled all:

> him all India obayd,
> And all that now America men call.
>
> [II.x.72]

Thus, from the beginning, myth has asserted what recent history proves: that the other world, now called the New World, was an original possession of the British imagination, and that that possession or mode of existence, Faery Land, is now called America. The ancient dream which must be revived in time is also the new-found place that must be refashioned in accordance with antique standards. In this double view of America, as once and future ideal, as original actuality and new potentiality, we have an emblem of how the poet's very act of retrospection, of looking back, is the act of restoration, of making up. For Spenser, as for so many others, to probe the past was to make the future, and America is a term for defining that process as well as an element in the process.

In viewing the New World as a potential revision of the antique world, Spenser also distinguishes the primitive, figured by the Indies or the Indians, from the antique, now new-found, figured by America. And he distinguishes between the primitive and the potential, because while the new may be primitive in some respect, the primitive is not necessarily new. He had to separate the New World from what had always been unshaped or unregenerate. Otherwise a sentimental equation between what was primitive and what was good would result, and in various ways the great Renaissance writers—all of whom worried this problem—resisted that widely held and much too easy conclusion.

So Spenser distinguishes between wild men and foundlings,[5] be-tween two orders of being—those who at best are susceptible of being tamed, and those who can be reformed. The distinction is crucial and wide-ranging, for it is between suppression and expression, domesti-cation and education, between beings who inhabit nature and beings who build cities. A wild man cannot change; the most one can hope to do is make him useful. A foundling, however, is precisely the image of potential change; at best, the process of civility is explicit in the education of the child.[6] In wild men, Spenser located what I have subsumed under the term "Indian," the primitive as fecund, ener-getic, but finally resistant; in the foundling, the new-found, he located what we have figured by "America," the ancient shape of man now new begun, the image of the past ready for rebirth. The distinc-tion, which points to self-consciousness, is about self-consciousness; it is a Renaissance distinction that, in its very assertion, reveals some of the Renaissance's deepest preoccupations.

By Spenser's wild men, I mean all the satyrs who receive Una at I.vi.7f. and who are received by Hellenore at III.x.36f; the "salvage" nations at VI.viii.35f; the grim forester who would rape Amoret at IV.vii.5; and the appealing wild man who rescues Calepine at VI.iv.2f. Obviously there are different kinds of satyrs and different levels of savagery. Amoret's pursuer and Serena's tormentors are far removed from Una's adoring host, and none of these approaches the decency of Calepine's rescuer who, when he knights himself by donning Calepine's abandoned armor (VI.v.8), seemingly completes or complements a series of affirmations in chivalry that began when Calidore reaffirmed Crudor (VI.i.42–43) and then dubbed Tristram as his squire (VI.ii.35). Indeed, this "salvage" man, as the poet says (VI.v.1), must have gentle blood; and in "salvage" the potential for salvation exists or seems to exist. But if Spenser recognizes the potential for improvement in the primitive order, he also recognizes that the potential is limited, limited because the primitive world has no self-consciousness, no self-reflexive vision. It has no art. It only has instinct. And good though instinct may be—it can be far better than what is misshapen by art, for instance—it is in itself not enough for true civility. All of Spenser's wild men finally derive from that very old tradition, superbly traced by Penelope Doob, of the sinful or bestial dweller in the wood.[7] They exist in Spenser's poem as images of fixed identity, beings who, much as their kind of energy is necessary to other orders on the chain of being, are still frozen at the bottom of that chain. Because they do not possess the capacity for self-transformation past certain limits, they will never pass from the woods to the city. These creatures inhabit the landscapes of Renaissance works as the final recalcitrant remnants of the medieval past, the last remnants of the romance and folklore world out of which so much Renaissance literature grew. They are remnants that refused transformation because they were so radically bound to that earlier world where all was meant to remain as it came from the Creator's hand. They are the primitive ancestors whom self-transforming Renaissance man has left behind, though—as Ariosto's Orlando so clearly shows in *Orlando Furioso* XXIII—they are what, when the process of civility defeats itself, the new man may instantly revert to. Wild men are what we have been and can be again if, as Spenser would say, we are "carelesse" (see Red Cross, "carelesse of his health, and of his fame," I.vii.7).

Broadly defined, however, foundlings represent the future; they project the material the process of civility works on, and the artifacts that result. Where wild men were medieval elements, man readymade, foundlings figure Renaissance hopes, man as he will be remade. The very terms *foundling* and *changeling* imply transformation and renovation: like America, they are terms for rebirth, a new start, a protean capacity to adapt the best of the past to the demands of the future. But because foundling and changeling can mean transformation as reformation, they can also figure deformation, something worse than wild because it could have been better. Spenser will treat foundlings from the benign or affirmative perspective, but we should remark that what is true of Renaissance men is always true of language: in the sixteenth century, both *foundling* and *changeling* had meanings that referred to shiftiness and deceit, particularly the deceitfulness of words.[8] Thus, only when a foundling is properly shaped, when the aesthetic fashioning is ethically or morally inspired, does the process of civility occur.

Who are the foundlings? In *The Faerie Queene*, there are two kinds: those who *were* foundlings, and those who *are*. The former list is very impressive, and includes Satyrane, Prince Arthur, Red Cross, Belphoebe and Amoret, Artegall, Tristram, and Pastorella—an extraordinary group that touches all the main concerns of the poem. Then there are the two infants: Ruddymane found by Guyon in Book II and the baby found by Calepine in Book VI. In fact, all books but the fourth present us with foundlings,[9] and a brief review of their origins and educations will show how and why Spenser stresses the status.

First is Satyrane, who as his name implies is closest to the order of primitives. He is introduced to the reader at the same moment as Una's satyrs to allow us to distinguish between the two types. The bastard son of a "lady myld" and a satyr, he was abandoned by his mother for his father to raise in the wild. Satyrane learned to subdue savage beasts, in effect overcoming the primitive part of himself (I.vi.21–26). And because he always considered his oppression of the beasts as "sportes and cruell pastime" (27), "bloody game" (29), and not as his only mode of survival—because in short his sense of play made him flexible and not, like the satyrs, fixed—he developed into the new man his father was not.[10] He became the "noble warlike knight . . . Plaine, faithfull, true, and enimy of shame" (20) who rescues Una. Satyrane is the emergent potential from (not of) the primitive past, and yet he only finds Una because he has returned to the wild "To seeke his kindred, and the lignage right, / From whence he tooke his weldeserved name" (20). As he does everywhere in his poem, Spenser here emphasizes genealogy, for the old energy cannot be reshaped in new forms unless it is first recovered. Spenser knows what his culture knows: that without exploring origins, we have no originals from which to fashion ourselves the new and true copies; that, for individuals as for institutions, unless one first returns to one's sources, *ad fontes*, there is no genuine rebirth. Satyrane is just over the line between primitive and civilized, a Janus who shows us in a shadowy way what the new man will be like, and where he has come from.

Once Satyrane establishes the paradigm for self-transformation in the foundling, Arthur and Red Cross reveal the type's full potential.

Both Arthur and Red Cross were stolen and raised by others: Arthur, stolen from his mother, is brought up by Timon, an old retired knight, and by Merlin (I.ix.3–5) (here all the models of action, contemplation, and flexible, benign magic are impressed upon him) for a great destiny which is only revealed (at least to us) in II.x when he reads *Briton Moniments*; Red Cross, a proper changeling left in a furrow, is reared by a ploughman under the name Georgos— the georgic one—for an epic future that is finally revealed by Hevenly Contemplation (I.x.64–66). Stolen too were Belphoebe and Amoret, twin daughters of Chrysogone, taken from their sleeping mother by Diana and Venus just after their birth. Belphoebe was then raised in the wild in "perfect maydenhed"; Amoret in the Garden of Venus and Adonis in "goodly womanhed" (III.vi.26–28). Renaissance eclecticism, taking what you need wherever you find it, is imaged in kidnapping.

Even Astraea had no qualms, evidently, about alluring "with gifts and speaches milde" the child Artegall and then raising him, like Satyrane, among the beasts where he learned "to weigh both right and wrong / In equall ballance with due recompence" (V.i.5–11). As we look back on the first time we saw Artegall, at IV.iv.39, in armor "like salvage weed, / With woody mosse bedight," and a motto *Salvagesse sans finesse*, we realize that he appeared so close to the primitive order, so very like the wild man in Book VI, because the poet was telling us how justice, based on primitive principles—the law of nature—is shaped for civic purposes with the most difficulty. And we also realize that the foundling who was so bound to the wild, so rough as a knight, signifies that Justice, the power that shapes others for civil ends, must itself incorporate primitive energies in order to be effective. In Book V, the image of that sense of force is Talus, the polished wild man.

In Book VI we meet the last two former foundlings. At VI.ii.27– 33, Tristram recounts his upbringing. Like Arthur and Red Cross, he was British born and raised in Faery Land; like Satyrane and Artegall, he was trained in manhood by tests in nature over beasts. The strands are beginning to come together. And finally, complement to Belphoebe and Amoret, there is Pastorella, abandoned by noble parents, found by the shepherd Meliboee (VI.ix.14; xii.3–22). She is the perfect heroine of old romance, at once aristocratic and rustic, ultimately restored to her parents at the end of Book VI—as Una had been at the end of Book I. Through the lost children of the poem, we are led to see that, for Spenser, civility is a process of passing through the primitive in order to engage it and thus consciously to overcome it. The primitive order does not give rise to civility; it only provides the backdrop against which civility defines itself.

This process of self-definition through self-transformation can only occur in a condition of displacement. The children were translated in order to be trained, removed in order that they could rediscover themselves or be reborn, because only by distance could they acquire the flexibility necessary for identity. Exile is the precondition for self-consciousness, culturally or individually. For instance, both Satyrane and Artegall are said, as lost children, to be exiled: Satyrane "from lawes of men exilde" (I.vi.23), Artegall, "from companie exilde" (V.i.6). In fact, all foundlings are exiles, and thus the process of civility involves both going out and coming back, displacement and homecoming, a removal from and return to the parents or shape one first had, return to the America that was Faery Land, return to the ethical norms and cultural forms of the classical world that, for the Renaissance, is the original model, the home new-found man has lost. [11]

Regardless of how this movement is viewed, whether in terms of an individual (foundling) or a culture (humanism), the sense of being exiled to achieve freedom and perspective—in order to transform yourself—means that the ethical process of civility is also a radically aesthetic process. The foundling is disciplined or nourished or shaped by antique mentors and ideals for a purpose, and the result is a different creation than would have occurred had the child (or culture) been left to grow naturally in a primitive state. All the foundlings noted above are examples of the process as it was long since begun or even completed. But in the two babies who are actually found in *The*

Faerie Queene, we can see the dynamics, not simply the results, of the process.

The first baby, Ruddymane, child of the dead Mordant and the dying Amavia, is rescued by Guyon at II.ii. 1 – 10. He tries to cleanse the child of its parents' gore, but the stains remain. The child is all of us, entering "Into this life with woe" (2), bearing the marks of our parents' sin. Even foundlings, the very images of potential change, are fixed in the ineradicable first condition of being fallen. Ruddymane is therefore the new-found in its harshest light, lost in the primitive wild, stained by sin, emergent, vulnerable. A canto later, leaving the hectic household of the mild Medina, Guyon gives her this child, conjuring her:

> In vertuous lore to traine his tender youth,
> And all that gentle noriture ensueth.
>
> [II.iii.2]

Ruddymane will be trained to remember the infamy of his parents and to avenge their deaths. He has a future, but it is determined by his origins, and, unlike the second baby's, Ruddymane's future is bleak.

Late in the poem, Spenser returns to the image of the baby, giving us (at VI.iv. 17 – 38), in a passage little noticed by commentators, the poem's most concentrated model for the ethical-aesthetic process of civility. [12] After being rescued by the gentle wild man, Calepine, alone, sees a bear with a screaming baby in its mouth. Again, as with Satyrane and the satyrs in Book I, the two orders of primitive and new-found are contrasted in a single canto. But in Book I we saw the foundling grown up and the primitive unregenerate, while in Book VI the foundling is newborn and the primitive as developed as it can be. In these parallel but reversed sets of images, we see the least and most in each order of being: the wild man is the most the satyrs will ever be, Satyrane is the least the foundling can become.

Calepine chases the bear, which turns in rage, dropping the child, and the knight rams a large rock down the bear's throat, choking it. In using nature (the rock) to overcome nature (the bear), Calepine does what certain foundlings (Satyrane, Artegall, Tristram) did. But even more, Calepine has used art. That is, he has turned the primitive world back on itself in a way the primitive order could never do itself. The result is that the nameless baby is freed from brute nature and taken up by Calepine, who finds him, despite all, "whole" (23). This baby is whole—or holy—that is, innocent still; he offers a different view of new-found things from that projected by the stained Ruddy-mane. Calepine, with his charge, now encounters a lamenting woman, Matilde, who tells how she and her husband Sir Bruin can have no children and how, without heirs, their hard-won land will revert to the giant from whom they first wrested it. Without a new future, all we have won from time threatens to collapse back into the primitive order. A prophecy, she says, promised they would have a son—*Be gotten, not begotten*—but age is beginning to overtake them. Renaissance is a constant imperative.

Calepine, perhaps the most nervous single parent in epic litera-ture, says it all—fast:

> If that the cause of this your languishment
> Be lacke of children to supply your place,
> Lo! how good fortune doth to yopresent
> This litle babe, of sweete and lovely face,
> And spotlesse spirit, in which ye may enchace
> What ever formes ye list thereto apply,
> Being now soft and fit them to embrace;
> Whether ye list him traine in chevalry,
> Or noursle up in lore of learn'd philosophy.
>
> And certes it hath oftentimes bene seene,
> That of the like, whose linage was unknowne,
> More brave and noble knights have raysed beene,
> As their victorious deedes have often showen,
> Being with fame through many nations blowen,
> Then those which have bene dandled in the lap.
> Therefore some thought that those brave imps were sowen
> Here by the gods, and fed with heavenly sap,
> That made them grow so high t'all honorable hap.
>
> [35–36]

In the second stanza above, Calepine tells Matilde that many "of the like, whose linage was unknowne," have become greater knights than those raised at home, and Satyrane, Arthur, Red Cross and Artegall come to mind. Specifically, Calepine's notion that foundlings are seeds sown by the gods and fed with "heavenly sap," with the thick, viscous light of divine ideals, recalls Red Cross, left "in an heaped furrow" (I.x.66). Here in the middle of Book VI, the central Christian virtue of Book I is recalled, as Courtesy fulfills Holiness, as—in Spenser's typology of foundlings—this nameless child completes and projects the pattern of Christian chivalry and civility first fore-shadowed in Red Cross. Finally, the imagery of divine seedlings reveals the organic basis of spiritual concerns and the way the art of civility is the process of mediation between natural energies and transcendent forms.

Art is what the process of civility is about, and art is what the first stanza cited speaks to: take this child,

> in which ye may enchace
> What ever formes ye list thereto apply,
> Being now soft and fit them to embrace.

You may transform the baby by applying whatever form you want, either chivalry or philosophy; you can shape him for the active or the contemplative life, says Calepine. The key word in the passage, and in Spenser's view of civility, is "enchace"; that word tells how you apply form to a baby or a culture, how you create reformation or renaissance. To "enchase" is the word that tells what an artist does.

In the sixteenth and seventeenth centuries, *enchase* meant to orna-ment; to set a jewel, to set gold with gems, to inlay or variegate metal with jewels, to adorn with figures in relief; to enshrine, to engrave. [13] And it was a word Spenser exploited throughout his career. In *The Shepheardes Calender, enchased* refers to a literal work of art, the traditional pastoral price, "A mazer . . . / Wherein is enchased many a fayre sight" ("August," 26–27). In *The Faerie Queene*, the poet refers to his own art: first, concerning Una's face:

> My ragged rimes are all too rude and bace,
> Her heavenly lineaments for to enchace.
>
> [I.xii.23]

Then, concerning many lovely faces:

> All which who so dare thinke for to enchace,
> Him needeth sure a golden pen, I weene.
>
> [IV.v.12]

And what the poet does was done to Alma's Castle, whose porch is "Enchaced with a wanton yvie twine" (II.ix.24); was done, says Scudamour, to the Shield of Love "With golden letters goodly well enchaced" (IV.x.8); was done, presumably by God's art, to "heavens bright-shining baudricke" which the twelve signs of the Zodiac do "enchace" (V.i.11).[14] What Calepine recommends to Matilde, that she enchase the child with whatever form she wishes, carries powerful and specific associations with the poet's view of the aesthetic process.

All the various kinds of artistic shaping implied by the word come home in the last use of *enchase* in the poem. Calidore has his vision on Mount Acidale; Colin Clout has conjured a hundred naked maidens around three ladies:

> And in the middest of those same three was placed
> Another damzell, as a precious gemme
> Amidst a ring most richly well enchaced,
> That with her goodly presence all the rest much graced.
>
> [VI.x.12]

"Enchaced"—"graced": what Calepine implied, Calidore, the Knight of Courtesy, sees in Colin's creation—the way the artist's power to make anew, rooted in nature, reveals divinity. Gloriously, if briefly, man is given insight into the way the process of civility redeems nature and therefore restores our heavenly origins. All men, all of us foundlings or exiles in the fallen world, are enchased, elevated, and humbled (chastened) by our vision through art of the paradisiacal home we lost in the race's infancy.[15]

Calepine's foundling, recalling all the earlier foundlings in the poem and projecting the vision on Mount Acidale, figures the process of civility: the radical alliance of aesthetic and ethical concerns that is the individual and cultural movement we call renaissance. The poet's last words on the baby are that Matilde and Sir Bruin raised him so well

> That it became a famous knight well knowne,
> And did right noble deedes, the which elsewhere are showne.
>
> [VI.iv.38]

A past tense reveals a future condition (precisely at the smallest syntactic level the movement of recollection for replication that we have been claiming occurs on the largest cultural level of the Renaissance). We never learn who the baby will be or what unwritten book he was meant to grace, but we are given to understand that the baby will also come home later in *The Faerie Queene*, that his future will be part of the constant process of redeeming and restoring the past. The once and future foundling, like the once and future America with which we began, projects the process of civility, at whose center is the artist who, by his morally informed power of mediation, recreates.

6

Marlowe: The Arts of Illusion

George Sabellicus was pleased to call himself, a contemporary tells us in 1507, "the younger Faust, the chief of necromancers, astrologer, the second magus, palmist, diviner with water and fire, second in the art of divination by water." But even this billing did not smooth the way, for Dr. Faust, as Sabellicus came to be called, was constantly forced to move on. City after city, nervously or defiantly, expelled him. It had always been so for the man called to the arts of illusion.

From antiquity through the seventeenth century, if no farther, the mummer, the mime, the juggler, the actor, the mountebank, the magician, even the scientist as astrologer or alchemist—all were suspect for their solitary or their irregular lives. But even more, they were profoundly distrusted for their varying and various capacities for irreverence. By irreverence, I mean not only their blasphemous conditions and conversation; I mean essentially their abilities to imitate and to transform, their gifts for changing shape and surpassing limits in ways which seemed to threaten divine plan or divinity itself. The historical Faust played to all these fears. By the time he disappears as an actual figure, around 1540, even his name has changed from George to Johann Faust—a harmless image within the historical records of his alleged sinister powers to manipulate appearances.

The Faust story is a product of the Protestant Reformation when, in Germany, men saw clearly the price of sin, the power of evil, and above all the limits of man. It was a time when the religious impulse, always ambiguous and now obsessed with purity and reform, precipitated out and identified its own darker side, the urge to magic and deformation. The Faust story is a Reformation story because it implies deformation as the result of any human impulse beyond or outside the strictly interpreted norm.

The Faust story sees both reformation and deformation as springing from the same source: the impulse to be at one with God—the difference being that the former results from submission to God, the latter from trying, like Faust, to assume godhead. But the Faust story has even deeper roots than the Reformation. It draws its radical potency from that great Renaissance (and hence modern) myth which says that spiritual reformation and deformation derive from man's innate power of formation, the capacity of the self to shape the self. The Faust story is firmly rooted in Renaissance man's profound conviction that he is a Proteus, that he can remake or change or transform himself.

The problem in this attitude, a problem crystallized by the Faust story, is this: Given man's basic urge and potential for transformation, would man reform himself in a good sense and be one of the blest, or would he deform himself and become a monster? What shape would he fashion for himself? Would he be Hyperion, or a satyr? Both were in him. Finally, once he unleashed the process of transformation, could he stop it? This was the most haunting question of all, and is the issue in *Doctor Faustus*.

> we must now perform
> The form of Faustus' fortunes, good or bad. [1]

So the chorus to Marlowe's play. And here Renaissance art offers itself as one solution to the massive ambiguities of Renaissance life. Performing is one way of forming, for the theater can safely release the human desire for new shapes. It provides an arena for limitless aspiration and multiple shapes while containing this impulse within the physical limits of the theater and the arbitrary structure of art. This is no final answer, because now the theater becomes simply a public image, a public language, for man's private agonies. "The great Globe" is a theatrical place and an individual's head, and both are reservoirs in their way for the energy to change and to remake human form. Both are dangerous places. The final solution is to purify the mind and the place; it is to have another Reformation, a Puritan revolution, and close down the theaters. You return to radical principles, write a poem justifying the ways of God to man, and go back to calling Faustus Satan or Eve. But that was all ahead. In the early 1590's, the theater was still being fashioned as the medium for manageable metamorphosis. And Marlowe takes a giant step when he transforms the material from the English translation (1592) of the German *Faustbuch* (1587) into a play about how the splendid urge to aspire to new form can deform past salvation if the shape you want is that of God Himself.

Renaissance man felt he had the power to transform himself because he had the power of language. Words were units of energy. Through words man could assume forms and aspire to shapes and states otherwise beyond his reach. Words had this immense potency, this virtue, because they were derived from and were images of the Word, the Word of God which made us and which was God. Used properly, words could shape us in His image, and lead us to salvation. Through praise, in its largest sense, our words approach their source in the Word and, therefore, we approach Him.

Because words, like men, were fallen, however, they contained, as we do, shapes of evil within them. Fallen words, like men, are unstable elements; thus they are, as we are, such dangers to us. As we must always check that impulse to deformation in ourselves, so we must constantly be aware of the beast in language—Spenser calls it the Blatant Beast, whose rabid bite is vicious slander—and we must know that when we unleash a word and let it soar, we run the risk of loosing an evil force as well, one that we cannot control. We, as men using words, must stay within our limits, or what we master may master and misshape us.

This is simply to say that the power of words and the power in words reflect our fallen state—above the beasts, below the angels, and capable of assuming either form. As a power, language is neither good nor bad. It all depends upon how we convert this energy, upon how we transform this power, in the mind with the mind. We are what we are depending upon how we shape ourselves with words; depending on whether we use words as God intended us to use them, or whether we use words to set ourselves up in His place and assume His knowledge and power.

Because all men are users of the magic power, language, because all men are performers with words and transformers through words, the Renaissance could figure all men under the single image of the *magus*, the magician. And as there were two ways of using language to project new shapes, a good and a bad, the Renaissance distinguished two kinds of *magus*. One is the "goetic" or black magician. This is Faustus, or Spenser's Archimago, or—in his own fashion—Iago, who imposes a nightmare on the island of Love, Cyprus, and who transforms the shape of Desdemona in the head of Othello. The other kind of *magus* and magic is represented by the "natural" or white magician. In harmless form this is Puck, who can take whatever shape he wants—"Sometime a horse I'll be, sometime a hound, / a hog, a headless bear, sometime a fire"—but whose power to transform finally will amend and harmonize all the divisions of love and the law. In Spenser's *Faerie Queene*, opposed to Archimago, there is Merlin in Book III who can project in his magic glass the true shape of love in Britomart's Artegall. Finally, there is the great white magician of Elizabethan literature, Prospero, who controls not only form and substance in Ariel and Caliban, and fashions justice and love, but who also can recognize the limits of his art and drown his book. This knowledge of white Prospero—where his knowledge stops—is acquired by black Faustus much too late.

In the black and white magicians, the Renaissance poets and thinkers saw concentrated the black dangers and the white glories of that single power, language, and that single urge, self-transformation. In the *magus*, they saw man; through the One, they perceived the

Many. Therefore Renaissance Faustus differs from all those other magicians who stand behind him in grand and receding array, Roger Bacon and Piero d'Albano (*Doctor Faustus,* I.i.155), the medieval Virgil (III.i.13), the sinister sorcerer Simon Magus, who offered to buy the power of the Holy Ghost (Acts viii.9–24; the apocryphal Acts of Peter), for Faustus is not simply doing tricks or trying to buy magic power. Faustus is any of us, any man using (and misusing) power in the quest for all knowledge and total control. Faustus is no trickster; he is modern man who would play the role of God.

In our play, the warring impulses for good and evil in the mind of everyman are visualized by the Good and Bad angels which hover around Faustus. Again, the single human head is the source for the double drive. And when we first meet those angels, the first words of the Good angel are:

> O, Faustus, lay that damnèd book aside,
> And gaze not on it. . . .
> Read, read the Scriptures. That is blasphemy.
>
> [I.i.71–74]

Here, at the outset, is an indication of the way the play is a battle of books. We see how the deepest issue in the play is words, the language of black magic versus the language of Scripture. We see how the power of words to shape for good or ill, and how that power is used and how that power can use you, is the pivot on which the play turns. We see how, at bottom, the problem of language remains.

Throughout his career, as he struggled to shape a new idiom for the nascent English stage, Marlowe wrestled with the multiform angel (or demon) of language. He made his problem as a playwright the subject of his plays. He expanded the limits of the stage by writing of the human mind in its battle to surpass human limitation. He used soaring words as symbols of man's aspiring mind. And he used the lurking dangers in words to image the terrors of aspiring too far.

Only *Doctor Faustus* fully exploits the glories and terrors in language to illuminate the full ambiguity of the human condition, though even as early as *Hero and Leander* one can hear Marlowe exploring through words the terrain of human potential, its mountain peaks and dark ravines:

> And fruitful wits that inaspiring are
> Shall discontent run into regions far.[2]
>
> [I.477−78]

In the earlier plays, however, the emphasis is heavily on man's mind as it soars beyond human limits—the dangers are not at issue yet—and thus the emphasis is on what language can do and not yet on what it can do to you. So we hear of the "aspiring mind" of Tamburlaine, and of his "conquering mind," whose foil is Bajazeth's "conquered head." Marlowe's great heroes all live in the present participle and the future tense. So in *Edward II* we hear of Mortimer's "virtue that aspires to heaven," but because we hear of it as he goes to prison, the ambiguities begin to emerge. And the ambiguities of the human condition are fully clear when we hear the Duke of Guise, whose "aspiring thoughts aim at the crown" (*The Massacre at Paris*, xix. 24):

> That I like best that flies beyond my reach.
> Set me to scale the highest pyramidès
> And thereon set the diadem of France;
> I'll either rend it with my nails to naught
> Or mount the top with my aspiring wings,
> Although my downfall be the deepest hell.
>
> [ii.42−47]

This is what the Marlovian hero always knows: his superb urge to transcend may also damn him deep.

Even more interesting is the image of Icarus submerged in the metaphor of flight in the last two lines. This myth fascinated Marlowe all his life, for like winged words themselves, it was another way of imaging the glories and terrors of transcendence. We first meet Icarus in Marlowe's earliest play, *Dido, Queen of Carthage*, when Dido passionately laments Aeneas' parting:

> I'll frame me wings of wax like Icarus,
> And o'er his ships will soar unto the sun,
> That they may melt and I fall in his arms.
>
> [v.i.243–45]

Dido will be Icarus so that she may fall, but later in the words of the Duke of Guise Marlowe exploits the myth as an image of the act of reaching per se and he comes back to Icarus one last time—if *Doctor Faustus* is his last play—in the chorus' description of Faustus, who excelled in theological disputes:

> Till swoll'n with cunning of a self-conceit,
> His waxen wings did mount above his reach,
> And melting, heavens conspired his overthrow.
>
> [Prol.20–22]

To say the Icarus myth has informed the substance of Marlowe's plays all along is a way of suggesting that Faustus, under various guises, has been all Marlowe's study. I am not implying Marlowe knew about Faust before he wrote of Faustus, though he may have, nor that Marlowe writes the same play over and over, for in crucial ways they are different. What I am suggesting is that in *Doctor Faustus* Marlowe's lifelong obsessions with the language of aspiration found their perfect vehicle. However, there is another sense in which *Doctor Faustus* reveals Marlowe's lifelong absorption in problems of language, and that emerges throughout the plays not in a Faust-like figure, but in a Faust pattern.

By Faust pattern, I mean that the crucial act in the Faust story is the consummation of a pact which promises a soul for twenty-four years of omnipotence. And in all the plays a pact or pledge has a critical role by representing that limit which the hero either rejects or overreaches. In *Dido*, it is the marriage pledge (Marlowe makes much of what his Virgilian source says is only a figment of Dido's imagination), which Aeneas superhumanly ignores to Dido's despair; in *I Tamburlaine*, there are Zenocrates' letters of safe conduct from the Great Cham himself which Tamburlaine, as his first act before us, countermands to prove himself "a greater man"; in *The Jew of Malta*, there are two pacts: the decrees Barabas refuses to sign which then deprive him of his goods (and goad him on) and the pledge between him and the Governor to betray the Turk, which both plan to break. In *Edward II*, the king is forced to sign a document banishing Gaveston, and in *The Massacre at Paris*, various pacts in the form of letters propel the Duke of Guise to his excesses, but none so much as the pledge of marriage—the "union and religious league"—between the king of Navarre and Margaret.

It would serve no purpose to push this pattern, if pattern it is, too hard. Still it is striking that in each play the hero defines himself and his role (or roles), his form and his performance, in terms of what for a better term we can call a verbal institution—some pact or pledge, letter, contract, or decree, whose validity as binding the hero at some point denies and which he tries to overcome. In all the plays, words supply a limit which the heroes' language attempts to supersede, an image of the mind trying to surpass our human limitations.

In *Doctor Faustus*, the verbal institution Faustus wants to overcome is language itself, language as it codifies, regulates, controls. And simply with his words, he can do this. He can send his words past the limits of other men's knowledge and control. But while his words are soaring, what about his deeds? What about the issue, the shapes, created by those flying words? If language is the power to form new realities, what are they? At the beginning of his career, with *Tamburlaine*, Marlowe saw no problem. "Go stout Theridamas; thy words are swords," says Mycetes. We change words to swords by prefixing an *s*, and for Tamburlaine things were almost that easy. He needed only to say he was a king to be one. In *Tamburlaine*, there is no gap between word and deed, no tragic lag between what you want and what you can have. But Tamburlaine is a figure of romance, the shepherd who becomes a knight and gets the girl. By the end of his career Marlowe had thought hard on our fallen state, and language; and tragedy, not romance, is the result.

In *Doctor Faustus*, the gap between word and deed widens and widens until it yawns like the mouth of Hell. As Faustus' language soars higher, the products of language—events, shapes, actions—become lower and lower, in the sense of trivial, in the sense of approaching Hell. What his words express and what they effect could not be more tragically separated. As we witness the widening gap between the mental spectacle the words conjure and the theatrical spectacle actually unfolding, between the way one thing is said and a very different effect is communicated or results, we see how Marlowe dramatizes the terrible ambiguities in the power of self-transformation through the magic of words.

First, the difference between what Faustus' words say and what his words actually do. In I.i we find Faustus alone in his study, about to "settle" his studies. He then speaks for some sixty-five lines. Now, according to his own words, he is a most learned man and very deep thinker; but according to what we see as a result of his words, Faustus has very patchy learning and a superficial mind. For while his words tell us he has soared above all organized human knowledge, they actually show us deep ignorance, particularly in the simple and central matters of the soul.

For instance, when Faustus dismisses Philosophy at line 10—he has attained its end; when he considers Medicine, finds it wanting, and dismisses it at line 27; when he says Law is all "paltry legacies," "external trash," and waves it away at line 36; and when he regards Theology and then, in the first of many unintentionally sinister puns (and there resides the issue of the play) bids it "adieu" at line 49—when he is saying all this, what do we actually see? When he says Philosophy is limited, we see a man who confounds Aristotle and Peter Ramus, a man who treats the deep questions of being and not being and the technique of disputing well as if they were the same. When he says Medicine is limited, we see a man who confuses gold and health, alchemy and physic, and who finds medicine wanting because it is not miracle, a lack he will remedy by turning to magic, miracle's parody. The soaring language does not offer us an ennobling spectacle; rather, the opposite.

When Faustus dismisses Law, something more sinister commences. To prove Law is really only legalism, Faustus quotes Justinian twice

in Latin. In the first citation, Faustus misquotes Justinian. But if the
ironic spectacle of misquoting what you claim is far beneath you were
not enough, further ironies attend the second citation, which is:
"The father cannot disinherit the son except . . . " (line 31). Faustus
leaves the citation unfinished, but the rest of the play completes it.
God the Father cannot disinherit man His son except when man
chooses to will his soul to Satan. What Faustus considers legalistic
trash far beneath his soaring mind is in reality an abiding principle
which eludes his grasp.

Nowhere does Marlowe's technique of having Faustus dismiss a
body of knowledge by a partial quotation have more devastating
effect than in Faustus' denial of Theology. Faustus says Theology only
teaches that we must sin and die, thus *che serà, serà*, and he wants no
part of a doctrine whose lesson is that necessity hangs over us.
Nowhere do we see his limitations through his statements of mastery
more clearly than here and in his citations from Scripture. He cites, in
Latin, Romans vi.23, "The wages of sin is death," but as with
Justinian's words he fails to finish the line: "But the gift of God is
eternal life through Jesus Christ our Lord." He cites the first Epistle
of John, "If we say we have no sin, we deceive ourselves, and there is
no truth within us," but he fails to finish the passage, "If we confess
our sins he is faithful and just to forgive us our sins, and to cleanse us
from all unrighteousness." It is certainly to convert, and abuse, the
power of the Word through one's own words when the Bible is
misshaped to justify turning to "heavenly," "necromantic books."
The play's techniques and issues are concentrated in this first speech
and projected into the rest of the drama. The more Faustus transforms
himself into a god through language, looking down on all human
experience and knowledge, the more we see his very words transform him into something foolish, ignorant, superficial; the more
Faustus tells of total mastery, the more we see a process of enslave-
ment. Finally, we begin to understand how Marlowe's irony operates
through the techniques of partial citation; for when Faustus only
partially quotes Justinian or the Bible, language releases a meaning
which Faustus does not pursue but which throughout the action of

the play pursues Faustus. That is the problem with language, and is
the issue Marlowe probes.

Faustus has dismissed Philosophy, Medicine, Law, and Theology.
He has embraced the "metaphysics of magicians." Then he exclaims:

> A sound magician is a demi-god.
> Here try thy brains to get a deity!
> Wagner—
>
> [63–65]

Here are those crucial lines where Faustus says in effect that through
magic he will assume powers only God has. Immense and potent
lines. Then, "Wagner"—and Wagner, his servant and disciple,
enters. The joke is verbally juxtaposing "deity" and "Wagner"; the
joke is visually juxtaposing mighty Faustus and foolish Wagner,
calling upon godhead and getting a goon. The terrifying implications
of this process (and scene) develop in Act II.ii, when Faustus cries out
to Christ, and Lucifer springs up. But that is tragedy, and later. This
is still funny—challenging Heaven and getting Wagner—and here,
in I.i, we really initiate the subplot.

The function of a subplot is to burlesque the concerns of a main
plot by mirroring those concerns in lower form; not simply to reduce
mighty concerns to absurdity but also to show us that no man's
mighty self is immune to human fallibility, to foolishness, to flaw.
The subplot is the great equalizer, savagely reducing or gently jesting
the main concerns as the dramatist sees fit. The subplot's ironic
spectacle and perspective make it a crucial element in *Doctor Faustus*,
and in Act I, Marlowe introduces us to its uses. In scene ii, Wagner
and the two scholars, but mostly Wagner, burlesque Faustus and his
two accomplices in magic in scene i; in scene iv, the actions of
Wagner and Robin, the clown, provide farcical, shrewd commentary
on Faustus and Mephistophilis in scene iii. In Act II, the subplot
begins to provide more than burlesque.

Scenes i and ii of Act II show us Faustus assuming the awesome
powers of the devil, and at the end of scene ii Lucifer gives Faustus a
gift: "peruse this book and view it thoroughly, and thou shalt turn

thyself into what shape thou wilt." But we really only understand the implications of this Satanic gift of words which shape when immediately in the following scene, Robin and Dick enter with one of Faustus' conjuring books. They mumble and jumble, parodying what has just preceded, and then make for a tavern where we meet them again three scenes later at Act III.iii. There, the vintner searches them for a stolen cup. Robin decides to conjure. And Mephistophilis appears. This is suddenly no joke. As Mephistophilis is the first to say:

> To purge this rashness of this cursèd deed,
> First be thou turnèd to this ugly shape,
> For apish deeds transformèd to an ape. . . .
> Be thou transformed to a dog, and carry him upon thy back.
>
> [40–42, 45]

The two clowns go off chattering and baying: in the devil's word, and by his word, transformed.

Here in the midst of farce, something serious has happened. The subplot's burlesque of the main plot's mighty concerns has been gradually acquainting us, in visual terms, with the way foolish shapes are latent in Faustus' aspiring words. But with the appearance of Mephistophilis at Robin's conjuring, this larger issue is clarified. We suddenly see clearly the way language releases meaning the user— here the clown—cannot control, and the way this meaning—here Mephistophilis—shapes or transforms the user. We see the transformer transformed, precisely what was suggested on the basis of Faustus' opening speech would happen to Faustus by the end. The seemingly simple contrast of subplot and main plot leads back to the central problem of the play: how the power to shape—language— can also misshape. And we have been led to this because the clown, transformed, is only a version of what Faustus, mighty magician, will become.

Or, indeed, what Faustus is rapidly becoming before our eyes. For there is that ever-growing split between Faustus' mighty words and his trivial deeds, between the shapes his language envisions and the shapes it actually creates. This larger movement, like the subplot which it parallels and meets in Act IV, begins in Faustus' second long speech in Act I.i, just after Wagner has appeared.

Beginning at line 79, we see the way Faustus' words fly up while their effects remain below. Faustus says he will create spirit servants. They will fly to India—for gold; ransack oceans—for pearls; search the corners of the earth—for fruits and delicacies. His servants will read him strange philosophies—and tell him royal secrets; they will dress schoolboys in silk, and invent new war machines. Here indeed is the language of aspiration—and the spectacle of naked appetite. Superb words—which show a taste for jewels, food, gossip, fashion, grim destruction. While we hear the flying words, we also see a man changing himself, through those words, from a magician to a dabbler in luxury to a general agent of death.

And when, over the course of the play, we see what Faustus does with those splendid powers; when we see how Faustus only uses them to vex the Pope and his retinue (III.i–ii), produce a dumbshow and put horns on a courtier (IV.ii), fool a fop with a false head (IV.iii) and a horse-courser with a false horse and leg (IV.v), and gather grapes for a pregnant Duchess (IV.vii)—then we see that what Faustus does with his power totally undercuts what we heard Faustus claim for his power. But not only does the power to be a god make trivia; much worse, that very power makes Faustus trivial. Over the play, the magician metamorphoses himself to a court jester, a fool. The process dramatized in the language of Act I.i is dramatized in the spectacle of the whole play.

The overall effect of this process is to trivialize everything, finally to trivialize main plot to the level of subplot. We see this happening when the characters of the subplot begin to enter the main plot— Wagner entering after Faustus gulls the horse-courser; Robin and Dick talking to the horse-courser and carter about Faustus' mighty deeds, like turning horses to hay. This merging of the two levels of life is completed in IV.vii when, after Faustus brings off his last piece of tremendous trivia—grapes for the Duchess—Robin, Dick, and company burst in and one by one Faustus charms them dumb. Now subplot is main plot; there is no difference. With his power to gain a deity, Faustus has reduced the world to its lowest level. Instead of learning the secrets of the universe, he has turned reality to farce. Finally, even the power of language, the power of transformation, is itself dramatically trivialized before our eyes when, without a word, Faustus denies the gulls the power of speech. That mighty power of language is so abused it no longer even communicates on a simple level; it only produces silence in the mouths of fools.

When we ponder the spectacle of the last scene, V.ii, in comparison with the statement of I.i, we notice that we see at the end precisely what we heard at the beginning. In both scenes, a universe, an unlimited existence, is unfolded. But, of course, similarities only underscore differences, and here the difference between the scenes is all the world. Where at the outset Faustus was a creator, at the end he is a creature; where before he dreamed of unlimited power and glory, now he is assured of limitless torment.

The words by which he reshaped himself into a demi-god at the beginning have now exploded into horror all about him. What we see on stage are the contents of his head—the Hell he will possess forever, the Heaven he will shortly lose. He brought it on himself, this deformed world, when he converted, when he turned to magic from God, when he turned to the power of words from God's praise to his own. It does him no good to shriek "I'll burn my books" at the very end. The power in his books has swallowed him, and he is now himself only a misshapen symbol, another occult sign, in Satan's ledger.

More than any other play, Marlowe's *Doctor Faustus* celebrates that God-like power of language, and shows us how words can soar, and tempts us to dizzying heights within our heads. But all the time, Marlowe is in control. He knows too much about the shaping power of words to be a Faustus. Marlowe is a *magus* too, all poets are, but one who tells us in this play to use that awesome power of words to fashion ourselves in God's image. Else, like his hero, we will be deformed by the servant we abuse.

7

Proteus Unbound: Some Versions of the Sea God in the Renaissance

Proteus, the sonne of Oceanus and Tethys, called of the paynimes the god of the sea whom Homere nameth to be the herde man of the fisshes called Phocae, and also a prophete, notwithstandynge he would not geue aunswere but beyng costrained by Ulisses. He also tourned himselfe into sundrie figures. Sometime like a bull, an other time like a terrible serpente. . . . In verie deede he was kynge of Aegypte in the time of Priamus kynge of Troy. Of him came the proverbe, PROTEO MUTABILIOR, more changeable than Proteus, applied to him that in his acts or words is unstable.

Sir Thomas Elyot, *Bibliotheca Eliotae*[1]

In 1518, the humanist and physician Ambrose Leo wrote Erasmus and compared him to Pythagoras and Proteus, the latter who "in varias formas mutasse sese, cum libuisset" ("changed himself into various forms, at will"). The comparison is apt because, says Leo to his friend, first you are in France, then you appear in Germany, then in Italy, in England, in France again, and then "de Gallo in Germanum transiisti" ("you have changed from a Frenchman to a German"). Leo quickly warms to his conceit: truly, he says, you change from poet to theologian, from theologian to cynic philosopher, and from cynic to orator: "quae mirae metamorphoses Protei illius solius videbantur" ("which marvelous transformations are like those of Proteus himself"). Now possessed by the spirit of his figure, Leo cannot resist one more variation:

Vidimus enim innumeros libros tuos impressos, quibus memoratas vel hominis vel ingenii personas et formas variasti . . . non vt vnus idemque sententiarum magnarum autor fores, sed tanquam tres quatuorue autores illarum essent.

For we see the innumerable books you have published, and in these works you so vary the character and aspect of the individuals and perspectives you recall . . . that you do not become one, single expounder of weighty maxims, but rather there seem to be three or four authors at work.[2]

In a genial reply from Louvain, Erasmus protests he has never been other than he is ("neq vnquam alius fui quam sum") and pointedly compares himself with Ulysses instead.[3] Perhaps Erasmus remembered, as his correspondent had not, that in his *Enchiridion* (1503) Proteus had figured the evil passions of man.

For an examination of Proteus in the Renaissance, two interesting themes emerge from Leo's homage to the great humanist and from Erasmus' evasion: first, that it was natural to signify man's potential for learning and virtue and, importantly, his artistic or literary capacities under the figure of Proteus; and second, that of all the interpretations of the shape-changer, some were by no means benign.

Other uses of Proteus in the Renaissance's image of man appear in a variety of thinkers. For instance, while in Louvain in 1518, Erasmus met the young Spanish humanist Juan Luis Vives, and shortly thereafter, Vives wrote his very suggestive *Fabula de homine*. To celebrate man, Vives tells of his playing various roles in the great theater of the world. Man assumes the guise first of plants, then many animals, and finally appears as himself—"prudens, iustus, socius, humanus, benignus" ("prudent, just, faithful, kindly, friendly")—he who lives in cities, creates and upholds laws, cares for the well-being of his fellow citizens, and is "denique nullus non erat civilis sociusque" ("finally in every way a political and social being"). The gods, astonished, proclaim him "multiformem illum Protheum Oceani filium" ("multiform Proteus, the son of the Ocean"); and when he first impersonates them, and then Jupiter, father of all, so that one cannot distinguish creator from creature, man is elevated to a place equal to the gods, a "brotherly guest or fellow citizen."[4]

In this Renaissance amalgam of classical and Christian, the figure of Proteus is crucial to the fable. Not only is Proteus appropriate to figure the multiple glories of man, but man's Protean ability to adapt and to act many roles is the source of the power that enables him to assume the burdens of civilization, to create cities on earth and win citizenship among the immortals. Man is not Protean because he is civilized; he is civilized because he is Protean, and the role of civic Proteus is central to the Renaissance's view of man in society.

Written after meeting Erasmus, Vives' fable owes much, of course, to Pico della Mirandola's famous *Oratio De Hominis Dignitate*. According to Pico, God gave man the central place in the universe, whence— unfettered—he may by his own free will choose whatever his nature will be.

> Tu, nullis angustiis coercitus, pro tuo arbitrio, in cuius manu te posui, tibi illam praefinies. Medium te mundi posui, ut circumspiceres inde quicquid est in mundo.

> You, constrained by no limits, in accordance with your own free will, in whose hand I have placed you, shall determine the limits for yourself. I have set you at the center of the universe, so you may survey from there whatever is in the universe.[5]

Man is given to be what he desires ("cui datum id habere quod optat, id essere quod velit"). Pico first compares him to the chameleon and then, following his Hermetic texts, to Proteus. For it was man, Pico says, who was symbolized by Proteus in the mysteries, and after examining the transformations found in Hebrew, Greek, and Islamic texts, Pico cites a Chaldaean saying which he translates thus: "idest homo varie ac multiformis et desultoriae naturae animal."[6] Why emphasize man as a creature "varied, multiform, and inconstant"? Because, he says, we must always remember the necessity to choose correctly, to be (and he quotes the 82nd Psalm) angels and not beasts.

As the *Oratio* unfolds, Pico becomes what he has described. For as he ranges through all human thought, he becomes a Proteus, a man with no native image but many appearances.[7] He says he is proud to be tied to no school, to no single doctrine, and to have known all forms of thought.[8] It is a superb boast, fulfilling the promise of Protean man set forth at the outset and revealing the way in which, through the forms of the Many, Pico is able to arrive at the One.[9]

Finally, as so often happens in the shimmering, shifting world of the Neoplatonic quest for unity, the subject and the object collapse into one another. This transference occurs at the end of the *Oratio*, as the material assumes its own Protean characteristics.

> Quod volui dixisse ut cognoscatur quis mihi labor, quae fuerit difficultas, ex affectatis aenigmatum syrpis, ex fabularum latebris latitantes eruere secretae philosophiae sensus, nulla praesertim in re tam gravi tam abscondita inexplorataque adiuto aliorum interpretum opera et diligentia.

> I wanted to say this so that it might be known what a task it was for me, how difficult it was to elicit the hidden thought of arcane philosophy from the studied tangles of riddles and the obscurity of fables, especially since in a matter so serious, so recondite, so little known, I have been aided by no experience or attention on the part of other interpreters.[10]

The image of Proteus, he who contains the truth under strange guises, now informs not only the knower but also what must be known.

If the figures of the chameleon and Proteus lead Ficino and Pico to the One behind the Many, over a century later the image of Proteus, submerged in the oceanic language of the *Essais*, would lead Montaigne to find the Many in the One: "chacque homme porte la forme entiere de l'humaine condition" ("each man bears the entire form of man's condition" III.ii).[11] Protean is the image for life: "La vie est un mouvement inegal, irregulier et multiforme" ("Life is an uneven, irregular, and multiform movement" III.iii). And for the best spirits: "Les plus belles ames sont celles qui ont plus de variété et de soupplesse" ("The finest souls are those which have the most variety and suppleness" III.iii).[12] And it is the image for himself, in whom

Montaigne finds the Protean quality of all human existence, with the result that he can only record the minute by minute change, the "metamorphoses" (III.ii) of growing old.

> Je peints le passage. . . . Je pourray tantost changer, non de fortune seulement, mais aussi d'intention. C'est un contrerolle de divers et muables accidens et d'imaginations irresoluës et, quand il y eschet, contraires; soit que je sois autre moymesme, soit que je saisisse les subjects par autres circonstances et considerations. [III.ii]

> I portray becoming. . . . I may change just now, not only by chance, but also by intention. This is a record of diverse and change-able occurrences, and of unresolved and—when it so happens—contradictory fancies; whether it be that I am another self, or that I grasp my subjects in different circumstances and see them in different lights. [13]

In such an undertaking, contradictions are inevitable, particularly because as in travel, so in all things: "la seule varieté me paye, et la possession de la diversité, au moins si aucune chose me paye" ("variety alone satisfies me, and the enjoyment of diversity at least, if anything satisfies me") (III.ix). [14] As life is his changeable element, so Montaigne is—one feels perforce—Protean in response; and if he is, so, in a celebrated passage, is man:

> Certes, c'est un subject merveilleusement vain, divers et ondoyant, que l'homme. Il est malaisé d'y fonder jugement constant et uniforme. [I.i]

> Truly man is a wonderfully vain, diverse, and undulating object. It is difficult to base any constant and uniform judgment on him. [15]

As in Pico, so here the Protean character of the investigator is also the primary characteristic of the object under investigation. But a different note is sounded in that "vain." The Florentine glory of man is here qualified, as all is qualified in Montaigne. The Protean language—man immersed in the ocean of life, an ocean of flux inhabiting man—carries an edge of melancholy, a sense of fatigue, the promise of futility. Now the limitless potential is also a curse. If man is Proteus, capable of all shapes, unfettered, as Pico has said, by any dogma—"Une seule corde ne m'arreste jamais assis" ("A single cord never holds me in place" III.ix)[16]—then he is also at the mercy of vanity and emptiness. None of us, Montaigne implies, Solon included, is exempt from the futility which attends this endless and necessary mutability.

The promise of humanism is proving false in the humanists' own terms. Where Pico or Vives had promised through Proteus angelic stature, an insight into single truth under multiple guises, a universe to command and enjoy, Montaigne knows that undulating diversity can also end in sheer waste: "Il n'en est une seule si vuide et necessiteuse que toy, qui embrasses l'univers" ("There is not a single thing so empty and destitute as you who embrace the universe"); and continuing, as if in reply to Pico's Protean knower and to Vives' Protean actor with his civic gifts, Montaigne can say of man: "tu es le scrutateur sans connoissance, le magistrat sans jurisdiction, et, après tout, le badin de la farce" ("you are the investigator without knowledge, the judge without jurisdiction, and, all in all, the fool of the farce" III.ix).[17]

Let us glance at one final Protean version of the human personality in the Renaissance. Robert Burton devotes the first part of his massive *The Anatomy of Melancholy* (1621) to the kinds, causes, and forms of melancholy, and at one point he finds Hippocrates and Galen proposing fear and sorrow as the disease's most frequent causes. But Diocles and Hercules de Saxonîa disagree, says Burton—the latter particularly:

> Four kinds he excepts, fanatical persons such as were *Cassandra, Manto, Nicostrata, Mopsus, Proteus, the Sybils*, whom Aristotle confesseth to have been deeply melancholy. . . . Demoniacal persons, & such as speak strange languages, are of this rank; some Poets; such as laugh always and think themselves King, Cardinals, &c. [I.iii, Mem. I, Sub. II][18]

Here Proteus takes on a darker hue, that of the black bile which, according to Aristotle, afflicted "all men who are outstanding in philosophy, poetry or the arts" (*Problems*, 953a). Melancholia, whether of the poet, lunatic, or lover, was a distinguished disease to have; but what is most interesting is that here Proteus, considered in his role as seer, is included with the "demoniacal persons" and their use of language and with the poets. As we shall see, Proteus will play those roles too.

From our brief glance at Renaissance versions of the self, two points emerge. First, the emphasis on Proteus, like the view of man, is never the same. Obviously the age's sense of man's ambiguous personality is admirably figured in that creature classical poets invariably called "ambiguus."[19] Second, implicit in all the roles Proteus would play in Renaissance literature would be Pico's view of him as a symbol for man's enormous potentiality. Indeed, this attitude, combined with the widespread idea that Proteus was, in Sir Thomas Browne's words, "the Symbole of the first matter," will survive into the nineteenth century; there in the second part of *Faust* Goethe will use Proteus as the vehicle for Homunculus in his quest for form and life.[20]

Besides the variations on Proteus as limitless man or as artist, an equally popular idea, our inquiry into Renaissance man has revealed another version of Proteus crucial to Renaissance literature. This is Proteus the lawgiver, or the civic Proteus of Vives; and because Proteus is nothing if not ambiguous, civic Proteus implies his opposite, Proteus the lawbreaker. This last form of Proteus is found in various guises everywhere—in the figure of the evil seer and the deceitful actor, both versions of the figure of the artist, as well as in his major role as violator of sexual norms and destroyer of cities and communal concord. Often Proteus will play several of these roles at once, hiding a malignant intention beneath a benign exterior. Thus he appealed to the Renaissance for many reasons, but above all two: because he could reconcile all differences and opposites, and because he embodied the principle of illusion as a mask for reality, appearance at once concealing and leading to vital or to deadly truths.

The time has come to make our move and to try to bind him. It will not be easy. The Middle Ages shows us the problem. It was divided on Proteus. In the ninth century, Theodulph of Orleans could assure his readers that Proteus meant Truth, while the *Roman de la Rose*, in Chaucer's version, associates him with "gile ne tresoun." In his spirit, the Renaissance will embrace both these and many other extremes. Proteus will appear before us successively in his guises of artist, lawbreaker, and lawgiver.[21]

To understand Proteus properly in his various roles as artist, it is necessary to see him first in his traditional role as seer or *vates*. This role originates in Homer where, in *Odyssey* IV (360–570), Menelaus tells how, on the advice of Proteus' daughter Idomethea, he tried to bind the god who appeared successively as a lion, snake, leopard, boar, water, and fire. (These became his standard shapes, as in Ovid, *Metamorphoses*, VIII.732–37.) Once bound, Proteus told him to honor the gods and then recounted the fates of Ajax, Agamemnon, Odysseus, and Menelaus himself.

Virgil's treatment of Proteus in *Georgic* IV was no less influential. There Cyrene advises woeful Aristaeus to consult the seer:

> Est in Carpathio Neptuni gurgite vates
> Caeruleus Proteus
>
> [387–88]
>
> In Neptune's Scarpantine gulf there is a seer,
> Proteus the sea god,[22]

—for he, like Yeats's bird, can sing of things past, passing, and to come:

> novit namque omnia vates,
> quae sint, quae fuerint, quae mox ventura trahantur.
>
> [392–93]

This episode, including the prophecy, ends the *Georgics* and establishes Proteus for later times as the ancient seer par excellence.[23]

The Renaissance constantly emphasized the prophetic powers of Proteus. Thus Boccaccio can begin his account in the *Genealogie* (VII.ix), "Proteus marinus deus, et insignis, ut aiunt, vates" ("Proteus was a sea god and, so they say, an eminent poet"), and then cite the fourth *Georgic* verbatim. Erasmus stresses Proteus as seer in the *Adagia*, as do Cooper in his edition of Elyot's *Bibliotheca*, Alciati in his famous book of emblems, and writers like Comes, Cartari, Bacon, and Ross in their explications of mythology.[24] There is a good reason for this interest in the seer, for in the Renaissance, the *vates* was also—as he would be for the Romantics—a general figure for the poet.

There is no need to stress this well-known idea. In his *Genealogie* (XIV.viii) Boccaccio follows Isidore of Seville and others in distinguishing between Moses and the prophets, who composed under the impulse of the Holy Ghost, and the secular poets. These last were impelled by a (Platonic) "vi mentis," an energy or power of the mind, and are therefore called *vates*.[25] Although there would be further refinements, Sir Philip Sidney sums up prevailing opinion in his *An Apology for Poetry* while reviewing terms for the poet:

> Among the Romans a Poet was called *vates*, which is as much a Diviner, Fore-seer, or Prophet . . . so heavenly a title did that excellent people bestow upon this hart-ravishing knowledge.

Later in speaking of the third and best kind of poet ("which most properly do imitate to teach and delight"), Sidney extends the term and makes it general:

> These be they that, as the first and most noble sorte, may be justly termed *Vates*, so these are waited on in the excellen[te]st languages and best vnderstandings, with the fore described name of Poets.[26]

As the casualness of Don Quixote's comment to the barber implies (II.i), this notion was the common property of all who thought or wrote about poetry in the Renaissance.

If Proteus was considered a prophet and *vates* was the common term for a poet, it is easy to see how the Renaissance could conceive of Proteus as a figure for the poet. In Sidney's celebrated description of the poet's nature, which occurs between his two statements on the poet as *vates*, we see the forging of this link:

Onely the Poet, disdayning to be tied to any such subjection, lifted up
with the vigor of his owne inuention, dooth growe in effect another
nature, in making things either better than Nature bringeth forth, or,
quite a newe, formes such as neuer were in Nature . . . so as hee goeth
hand in hand with Nature, not inclosed within the narrow warrant of
her guifts, but freely ranging onely within the Zodiack of his owne
wit.[27]

The Protean implications reside in the humanist idea of man free to
grasp the universe with his mind, in the exalted status of the poet and
his superior powers, qualities implicit in the vatic powers of Proteus
and often attributed to him,[28] and finally in the language itself. For
the poet, able to teach and delight, is like Proteus unfettered—
"disdayning to be tied to any such subjection"—freely creating his
version of things, constantly growing ". . . another nature."

This brave notion of the Protean writer who knows many things
and can assume various forms through and of expression is one we
have met before. It was explicit in Leo's encomium of Erasmus'
multiple literary talents; it was implicit in Pico's and even Montaigne's vision of their writing and knowing selves as Protean; it was
hinted by Burton's inclusion of Proteus (and other seers) with the
poets. Finally it is stated clearly by Comes in his account of Proteus:

> Alii, inter quos fuit Antigonus Carystius in Dictione, Proteum virum
> sapientissimum fuisse tradiderunt, qui multa de naturali philosophia
> scripserit, de plantis, de lapidibus, de natura ferarum, di mutatione
> mutua elementorum. [*Mythologiae*, p. 854]

> Some writers, for example, Antigonus Carystius in his *Dictio*, related
> that Proteus was a most wise man, who wrote a great deal about
> natural philosophy, about plants, stones, the nature of wild animals,
> and the mutual transformation of substances.

Later, under the name of Proteus, Edmund Waller can laud both a
poet and his plays:

> The sundry Postures of thy Copious Muse
> Who wou'd express, a thousand Tongues must use;
> Whose Fate's no less peculiar than thy Art,

For as thou cou'dst all Characters impart,
So none cou'd render thine, who still escap'st
Like Proteus in variety of Shapes:
Who was, nor this, nor that, but all we find
And all we can imagine in Mankind.

["Upon Ben Jonson"]

Proteus as a figure for the writer's plenitude and grasp of all experience would survive to the nineteenth century, where a French novelist fighting the wars of realism will say: "L'idéal pour un romancier impersonnel est d'être un protée, souple, changeant, multiforme, tout à la fois victime et bourreau, juge et accusé." ("The ideal for a realistic novelist is to be a Proteus, pliant, changing, multiform, at once victim and executioner, judge and accused.")[29]

While it is true that classical literature offers no direct precedent for identifying Proteus and the poet, to the Renaissance mind ranging the zodiac of its wit the fact that Virgil's *vates* in *Georgic* IV tells Aristaeus the story of the archetypal poet Orpheus must have been suggestive.[30] And certainly one figure of the poet in classical literature was associated in the Renaissance with Proteus. That was the shepherd poet, the singer of pastoral. From Homer on, Proteus had been the keeper of the sea creatures. A reference to him justifying the shepherd's calling in Theocritus (VIII.52) and a simile comparing him to a shepherd in *Georgic* IV (433–36) must have validated Proteus' pastoral credentials, for they were certainly in order for Comes, who grandly saw him as a type of the "populorum pastores" ("shepherd of nations"). To Spenser, he was simply the

shepheard of the seas of yore
[Who] hath the charge of Neptunes might heard.

[*Faerie Queene*, III.viii.30][31]

The fact that Proteus was a shepherd by itself did not necessarily link him with the poet-shepherd of pastoral. That final connection was made by the Renaissance poet uniquely suited to appreciate and exploit Proteus' marine duties. I refer, of course, to Jacopo Sannazaro, creator, he claimed, of the piscatory eclogue.[32] In his *Ecloga* I

(Phyllis), Sannazaro calls Proteus "divino pectore vates" ("a poet with divine insight" 88) and thus echoes Virgil's *Eclogue* VI, "divino carmine pastor" ("shepherd of divine poetry" 67).[33] This is most interesting because of *what* is being echoed. Virgil's phrase occurs in a passage on poetry (64–73) and refers to Linus, who with Orpheus, Musaeus, and Arion was considered in antiquity and the Renaissance as one of the fathers of poetry. Thus Sannazaro's Proteus, "the seer divinely inspired," refers specifically to the great poet-"shepherd of immortal song." But the possibilities of Proteus as pastoral poet are still not exhausted for Sannazaro, who seems to take Proteus' shepherding for granted. For who is singing of Linus in Virgil's sixth *Eclogue?* It is the god Silenus who, says Virgil, had to be caught when asleep by Chromis and Mnasyllos and fettered with his own garlands (15–19) else he would not sing. Silenus, already identified in the Renaissance with Proteus because both embodied truth under strange exteriors, here bears a striking resemblance to the sea god who would not prophesy until bound.

Sannazaro exploits these possibilities to their fullest in his *Ecloga* IV *(Proteus)*, where Silenus' song of creation becomes Proteus' celebration of the Bay of Naples and its environs and where all of Virgil's *Eclogue* VI is imitated down to its smallest detail. Sannazaro even widens his scope in this poem to include by allusion other Virgilian singers and his own previous references to Proteus as a poet.[34] Proteus is now so completely a poet for Sannazaro that in a *canzone* he will have Proteus simply arise from the sea, immutable no less ("più non si cangia di sua propria forma"), and sing the praises of a nameless lady like any other self-respecting *cinquecento* versifier.[35]

When Comes alludes to Proteus' marvelous power with words— "Alii dixerunt fuisse virum dicendi peritum, qui facile posset in quovis animorum motus homines impellere" ("Some said that he was an accomplished orator, who could easily sway men in any direction he pleased")[36]—he is only generalizing on the tradition we have traced. The concept of Proteus as poet, whether as a result of his role as *vates* or as shepherd, has been a benign one. He has shared and embodied the exalted status of the poet as the free imitator of nature and maker of forms, as the diviner of secrets and the possessor of valuable truths. With Proteus, however, ambiguity is the norm, and the other, darker side of Proteus' power with words is an important dimension in his role in Renaissance literature.

In the Renaissance, the power to manipulate words carried awe-some responsibilities. As words could create, imitate, and ennoble, they could also falsify and deceive, projecting illusions which bore no necessary relation to actuality. Furthermore, words were notoriously unstable, in this way a true image of human affairs, which were also seen as constantly in flux. Words as a medium for illusion and as unstable, the image of mutability, found their proper counterpart in Proteus, who was archetypally both deceitful in his various disguises and the very quintessence of change. Therefore, Proteus' various roles as a manipulator of words must be seen as they were colored by the deceptive and mutable possibilities inherent in him and in language.

The link between the darker elements in Proteus and in words is magic. As Proteus' role as *vates* had allied him with the beneficent figure of the poet, it also associated him with the often sinister *magus* or magician. In his *Oratio*, Pico had distinguished two kinds of magic. He referred to both kinds as "artes" but says one is the most deceitful of arts, the other the best; one makes man a slave of evil powers, the other makes him their lord and master. Finally, one damns, the other saves:

> Ob hoc praecipue quod illa hominem, Dei hostibus mancipans, avocat a Deo, haec in eam operum Dei admirationem excitat, quam propensa caritas, fides ac spes, certissime consequuntur.

> For this reason especially: that the former, in delivering man up to God's enemies, calls him away from God, while the latter rouses him to that admiration of God's works which most surely leads to a willing faith, hope, and charity.[37]

Though Proteus is nowhere explicitly mentioned in this discussion of magic and its practitioners, he was certainly widely regarded as a *magus*, as both Tasso and Milton attest, and as one possessing certain (magic) arts. Perhaps echoing the reference in Virgil when Proteus begins to change shape—"ille suae contra non immemor artis" ("but he was not unmindful of his art" *Georgic* IV.440), Comes says that "Alii crediderunt per magicas artes Proteum in praedictas formas se mutasse" ("Some believe that it was by magical art that Proteus took on the shapes I have described").[38]

Though there is nothing necessarily sinister in the imputation of magical power to Proteus, the potential for evil is there. Again Sannazaro exploits the possibilities. In the sixth eclogue of the *Arcadia*, the shepherd Serrano laments the passing of the Golden Age and demonstrates the depravity of the present by telling how a shepherd came to his door, tricked him into injuring himself, stole two kids and two goats, and then had the effrontery to boast of his crime before spitting three times and disappearing. "Questo è Proteo," says the much-abused Serrano, and though the passage again identifies Proteus with the shepherd, here he is no singer. Rather he is a perfidious magician, as Serrano's catalog of his tormentor's luggage proves:

> Erbe e pietre mostrose e sughi palidi,
> ossa di morte e di sepolcri polvere,
> magichi versi assai possenti e validi
> portava indosso, che 'l facean risolvere
> in vento, in acqua, in picciol rubo o félice;
> tanto si può per arte il mondo involvere.
>
> [46–51][39]

> Herbs and monstrous stones and dread juices,
> Bones of the dead and the dust of tombs,
> He carried about very strong and efficacious
> Incantations, which made him dissolve
> Into wind, water, or into a small bramble or fern;
> So much can the world be deceived by art.

Here the "arte" is indeed that of the evil *magus*, though Sannazaro's polished, languid verses make Proteus sound more like a Neapolitan Puck. The most interesting trick in his bag are those "magichi versi assai possenti e validi," for they begin to reveal the link between

Proteus and a long tradition concerned specifically with his ability to manipulate and distort words. From this tradition, the dark side of the benign poet will emerge.

Plato first equates Proteus with devious manipulators of words in the *Euthydemus*. There Socrates says of the two Sophists Euthydemus and his brother Dionysodorus: "They do not care to give us a serious demonstration, but, like the Egyptian wizard, Proteus, they take different forms and deceive us by their enchantments" (288c).[40] Proteus' wizardry is specifically the source of deceit and, through the Sophists, his magical powers are associated with the misuse of words. The same point is made at the end of the *Euthyphro*. Euthyphro's circularity on the question of piety finally exasperates Socrates, who asks:

> And when you say this, can you wonder at your words not standing firm, but walking away? Will you accuse me of being the Daedalus who makes them walk away, not perceiving that there is another and far greater artist than Daedalus who makes things that go round in a circle, and he is yourself. [15c]

and he then compares Euthyphro specifically with Proteus (15d). Through association with the great and cunning artist Daedalus and the unintentionally sophistic Euthyphro, Proteus is firmly implicated in the walking words—language as it serves ends other than the truth.

In their accounts of Proteus, Renaissance mythographers were not slow to echo and to elaborate on these Platonic hints.[41] In the meantime, another classical source confirmed Proteus' association with sinister, magical manipulation of words. In Petronius' *Satyricon*, the witch Oenothea praises the power of words after her own fashion. "Tantum dicta valent" ("so great is the power of words"), she says, for a virgin can calm the fiery spirit of a bull:

> Phoebeia Circe
> carminibus magicis socios mutavit Ulixis,
> Proteus esse solet quicquid libet. His ego callens
> artibus Idaeos fructives in gurgite sistam
> et rursus fluvios in summo vertice ponam.[42]

> Circe, child of Phoebus,
> transformed Ulysses' comrades with magic spells;
> Proteus is wont to be whatever he wants. Cunning
> in these arts, I can plant in the sea the bushes of Mount Ida,
> or turn rivers back on mountain peak.

Oenothea's power to pervert nature, Circe's to change men, and Proteus' to shape himself are all evidently the result of demonic powers exercised through language.

Fully as interesting for the Renaissance as Proteus' ability to make words control and distort things is his association here with Circe, an association which parallels the way he was linked with Silenus in benign roles. For once Proteus falls within Circe's orbit, he is allied with a figure who exercised an enormous fascination for Renaissance poets, as Ariosto's Alcina, Tasso's Armida, Spenser's Acrasia, and others testify, and his own demonic potential is strengthened by the association.[43] Tasso, for instance, sees the link between Circe and Proteus in his *Gerusalemme Liberata*. At Armida's first appearance in the Christian camp, she manages "e far con gli atti dolci e co 'l bel viso / più che con l'arti lor Circe o Medea" ("to accomplish more with grace and a lovely smile, / than Circe or Medea could, with all their arts" IV.86), while later, "Tentò ella mill'arti, e in mille forme / quasi Proteo novel gli apparve inanti" ("She tried a thousand spells, and in a thousand shapes / appeared to him as a sort of second Proteus" V.63).[44] In both cases, whether Armida is seen as Circe or Proteus, her "arti" are at issue, those deceitful arts which Pico had said could estrange man forever from God.

Thus parallel to the tradition of Proteus as *vates* and poet is a tradition of Proteus as *magus* and sinister manipulator of words. The two traditions support one another, providing reciprocal tension and balance, for each depends on the other for the reservoir of ambiguity that gives Proteus, and language, the potency to adapt and to signify. The mutual dependence, or interpenetration, of the demonic and the divine elements in Proteus tells us something about the Renaissance and its view of language. Even more is said about the Renaissance itself when we notice that the demonic Proteus, the potential for chaos, falsity, and death, predominates.

In 1675 *Proteus Redivivus: Or the Art of Wheedling, or Insinuation* appeared in London, a cynical and entertaining book which pretends to teach the young how to succeed in society while it poses as an exposé of the vices of the times. In adopting the figure of Proteus, the author makes a serious point which bears directly on those dark powers of Proteus to manipulate words. The art of wheedling is defined as the

> *Art of Insinuation*, or Dissimulation, compounded of mental reservation, seeming patience and humility, (Self-obliging) civility, and a more than common affability, all which club to please, and consequently to gain by *conversation*,

and shortly the author observes that the

> *Protei* of this loose age can turn themselves into any shape, so that the *conversion* of the form will produce any profit or advantage.[45]

I have italicized "conversation" and "conversion" because these words, sharing a common root in the Latin "convertere," to turn or to transform,[46] reveal how the changeable nature of language was associated with Proteus and with the power he had, which was to deceive. Words change, like Proteus; he is able to deceive by changing, and one of the ways he does it is by manipulating words. Thus he is an image for the demon in language and for the user of language for demonic purposes.

Such comments may seem to read too much into the bantering tone of the *Proteus Redivivus*, but the demonic powers in and of language and their association with Proteus had already been seriously noted and explored in English literature by the end of the sixteenth century. We have only to turn and note the uses of language in *Doctor Faustus* and *The Faerie Queene*.

Faustus knew well that there were times when one must

> Be silent then, for danger is in words.
>
> [V.i.25][47]

But long ago he had succumbed to their power:

> Valdes, sweet Valdes, and Cornelius,
> Know that your words have won me at the last
> To practice magic and concealed arts.
>
> [I.i.101–03]

The magical properties in language make Faustus a great magician; after his first Latin incantation, Mephistophilis appears. Faustus's first words to him, however, are:

> I charge thee to return and change thy shape,
>
> . . .
>
> Go, and return an old Franciscan friar;
> That holy shape becomes a devil best.
>
> [I.iii.23–26]

Mephistophilis leaves, shortly to return at Faustus's command, and the *magus* is pleased the devil is so "pliant" (29). The humor here masks something more serious. Faustus thinks he has unlocked the demon by language, that his words can control the devil's shapes, but the terrible irony is that Faustus has also unlocked the demon *in* language—a demon who, like Proteus, can change shapes. Throughout the play, while Faustus thinks he shapes his own future with his magical words, the words are actually shaping the destiny of his soul. When Mephistophilis provides Faustus with words, Faustus believes he will have power over all men:

> Hold; take this book; peruse it thoroughly . . .
> Pronounce this thrice devoutly to thyself,
> And men in harness shall appear to thee,
> Ready to execute what thou command'st.
>
> [II.ii.157, 161–63]

Like Pico's evil *magus*, however, upon whom the play is in a sense a gloss, Faustus is really the slave of the power he commands and is finally estranged from God.

Lucifer himself even gives Faustus a book:

> view it thoroughly, and thou shalt turn
> Thyself into what shape thou wilt
>
> [II.iii.168–69]

as Marlowe, in a profound insight into conversation implying conversion, identifies the Protean character of the *magus* with the demonic force in words. Words have their origin in that Word which was God, and whoever tampers with this divine gift by assuming demonic powers will be assumed by those powers and will have his form altered by the demon in the words. Marlowe's irony derives from the fact that, for all his learning, Faustus is ignorant in the matter of salvation.

Spenser's Archimago, however, is no such innocent. This great wizard, explicitly identified with Proteus, knows precisely what he is doing or thinks he knows. Through him we gain even deeper insight into the demonic Protean power of words and the dangers, even for the *magus*, of using them. Archimago's powers are displayed in the first canto of *The Faerie Queene*. His "pleasing wordes" (35) lure the Red Cross Knight and Una to his house to pass the night. Once they have retired, he consults "his magick bookes and artes of sundrie kindes" (36), chooses a "few wordes most horrible, (Let none them read)" (37), and out of "deepe darkness dredd" (38) conjures two false sprights, one who descends to the Cave of Sleep for "a fit false dreame" (43), the other whom Archimago fashions into a false image of Una to deceive the Knight. But even after Red Cross has been divided from his lady, Archimago vows to work Una further harm:

> He then devines himselfe how to disguise:
> For by his mighty science he could take
> As many formes and shapes in seeming wise,
> As ever Proteus to himself could make:
> Sometime a fowle, sometime a fish in lake,
> Now like a foxe, now like a dragon fell.
>
> [I.ii.10]

This passage looks back to the whole tradition of the *magus* and Proteus' associations with him, and Spenser will later apply the imagery of Proteus again to his magician (I.xii.35; II.i.1). However, this episode will yield more.

As we know, the poet bade none read the "verses" Archimago originally framed (I.i.37) in order to summon the false sprights from the deep. There seems a hint here of the forces in language which the poet, creating this dream world of the poem, knows better than to tamper with—nightmare forces, which only Archimago, false creator or poet of darkness, whose muse is "Great Gorgon, prince of darknes and dead night" (37), can handle. Yet even Archimago is subject to terror, for at the end of the stanza identifying him with Proteus, we learn:

> That of himselfe he ofte for feare would quake,
> And oft would flie away. O who can tell
> The hidden powre of herbes, and might of magicke spel?
>
> [I.ii.10]

A good question, which is answered by the whole poem where the forces here out of control are constantly subjected to that ceremonious control of the poet and the good government, within and without, of the various heroes. But the power in language and those powers unleashed by language demand constant vigilance and can never be totally checked, just as in *The Faerie Queene* there are potent, demonic forces which can never be entirely curbed—the forces represented by Duessa and Malbecco, for instance, both expelled from society but neither extinguished; the powers of the Dragon, who can never be killed; of the Blatant Beast, who cannot be tied down; of Archimago himself, who disappears from sight but who, we assume, continues to roam the world; or, finally, of Despair, a central figure in the poem, whose own medium is words (I.ix.48, 53) and who cannot die until the Last Day, when all will be at peace.

I seem to have digressed, but, like the poet, with a purpose. That was to suggest that Spenser was profoundly aware of forces in human nature which would be a constant danger to man, that these forces lurked in that power which distinguished man from beasts—language—and that one could see the beginnings of Spenser's development of this theme in the Protean figure of Archimago, a type of the poet who could appeal to but not control the Protean potency in and of words.

There is one final exploitation of Proteus as poet and *magus* in alliance with the potential of language, and that occurs in *The*

Dunciad of Alexander Pope. Here Proteus figures those poets and writers whose words corrupt. These writers corrupt, however, not because, like Faustus or Archimago, they appeal to the demonic forces in language. Rather these men have no sense of the divine origins of language or of the proper use of words to create and civilize. Thus through their ignorance their words invariably destroy, creating monsters instead of the proper image of man and spreading chaos instead of light.

Near the beginning of Book I, we read that from the Cave of Poverty and Poetry,

> Hence Bards, like Proteus long in vain ty'd down,
> Escape in Monsters, and amaze the town.
>
> [I.37–38][48]

Were there any ambiguity about the identification of the targets of Pope's lash, it was dispelled in Warburton's note. There, after citing Ovid (*Metamorphoses* VIII. 730–34) on Proteus' changes into a boar, a snake, a bull, and a stone, Warburton says "Neither Palaephatus, Phurnutus, nor Heraclides" can elucidate this mysterious myth. With that jab at scholarship, he then provides some of his own:

> If I be not deceived in a part of learning which has so long exercised my pen, by *Proteus* must certainly be meant a hacknied Town scribler; and by his Transformations, the various disguises such a one assumes, to elude the pursuit of his irreconcilable enemy, the Bailiff. Proteus is represented as one bred of the mud and Slime of Ægypt, the original soil of Arts and Letters: And what is a Town-scribler, but a creature made up of the excrements of luxurious Science? By the change then into a *Boar* is meant his character of a *furious and dirty Party-writer*; the *Snake* signifies a *Libeller*; and the *Horns of the Bull*, the *Dilemmas* of a *Polemical Answerer*. These are the three great parts he acts under; and when he has completed his circle, he sinks back again, as the last change into a *Stone* denotes, into his natural state of immoveable Stupidity.

The effect of these Protean hacks is to "amaze the town," that is, by their writing to introduce into the human community a kind of confusion which finally reduces the city to chaotic wilderness. However, the poison seen as introduced into the City, either in this couplet or in the processive movements to the Temple of Dulness in the poem as a whole, is but an analogue to the poisoning of the mind, seat of the city within and source of the power with which to civilize without. Here the reference to the Protean bards as Monsters finds its true meaning, for as their misuse of language fills the city with monstrous shapes, so these perversions are but reflections of what their ignorance has already done to them. The Queen explains it to Dulness:

> Son; what thou seek'st is in thee! Look, and find
> Each Monster meets his likeness in thy mind.
>
> [III. 251–52]

The Protean perversion of shapes becomes not only an emanation from but a symbol for the perverted imagination which, misusing the power originally in the Word, spreads horror and chaos instead of order and light.[49]

The final echo of Proteus occurs at the commencement of the decay in civil order, Silenus announces to the Queen that her "Magus" (IV.516) will preside: "With that, a WIZARD OLD his *Cup* extends" (517). "Here beginneth," Warburton explains, "the celebration of the *greater mysteries* of the Goddess" where, under the influence of the wizard's libation, "each of the Initiated . . . putteth on a *new Nature*." Proteus had been called the "*Carpathian* wizard" by Milton in *Comus* (872), the same work in which Milton also referred to the "charmed cup" of Circe (50–51). And here a *magus*, with Proteus' (and Circe's) power to change shapes, presides over the final dissolution, a dissolution not only of all human forms but of all human and divine ties, hierarchies, order. For as Pope's and Warburton's note glosses the end of the line:

> The *Cup of Self-Love* . . . causes a total oblivion of the obligations of Friendship, or Honour, and of the Service of God or our Country; all sacrificed to Vain-glory, Court worship, or yet meaner considerations of Lucre and brutal Pleasures.[50]

The monstrous Protean perversion of language will usher in the kingdom of the "uncreating word" (IV.654) and the black arts of the *magus* create the "Universal Darkness" (656) whence they come.

At the outset of our binding of Proteus, I claimed he had various guises under the general mask of the artist. And besides the ambiguous conception of him as *vates*-poet, which only concealed his darker role as *magus* and demonic manipulator of words, the Renaissance also distinguished Proteus the actor, a role which will reveal him essentially as a seducer. From that version, we will easily see the origins of Pope's use of Proteus as a force hostile to civilization, for the deceiver leads naturally to the lawbreaker.

The general idea of Proteus as a deceiver is a basic element in all accounts of the god. In Homer, for instance, Idomethea deceives her father by telling Menelaus his secret; Menelaus disguises himself in a sealskin; Proteus tries to deceive Menelaus by changing shape. The specific image of the actor stems from this general theme, though as in the version of Proteus the poet, there can be wide variations in emphasis. In Vives' *Fabula*, for instance, Protean man was explicitly conceived as an actor, and this ability to mimic and adapt won him a seat of honor among the gods. Marlowe could also use Proteus positively to praise the great Edward Alleyn:

> Whom we may rank with—doing no one wrong—
> Proteus for shapes and Roscius for a tongue,
> So could he speak, so vary.
>   [*The Jew of Malta*, Prologue to the Stage, 9–11]

Others would speak of Proteus as actor or performer neutrally, with neither sinister nor beneficent implications. As Lucian, in a passage noted by Renaissance mythographers, did in his dialogue on *The Dance*:

> For it seems to me that the ancient myth about Proteus the Egyptian means nothing else than that he was a dancer, an imitative fellow, able to shape himself and change himself into anything, so that he could

imitate even the liquidity of water and the sharpness of fire in the liveliness of his movements.

In the same neutral vein, Tasso ingeniously uses Proteus as an actor by introducing him as the scene-changer in the interludes written for *Aminta*.[51]

But as before, the associations of Proteus with deception and evil predominate, and again Plato provides the ultimate impetus. Now we turn to the *Ion*, where the (self-confessed) best rhapsode in Hellas has also admitted he is the best general. Socrates accuses him of deception (541e), as the typical Platonic technique of making the dialogue enact what it discusses unfolds. The rhapsode, earlier associated with the actor and poet as links in the chain whereby God "sways the souls of men in any direction which he pleases" (536), now practices the deception of avoiding Socrates' logic and his own promises. As before with the Sophists, Socrates is annoyed:

> You literally assume as many forms as Proteus, twisting and turning up and down, until at last you slip away from me in the disguise of a general, in order that you may escape exhibiting your Homeric lore.
> [542]

In the Renaissance, the sinister implications of Proteus the actor are exploited, naturally enough, in the drama. Indeed, two recent discussions of sixteenth- and seventeenth-century drama have begun with the figure of Proteus, emphasizing his importance for the controlling ideas of deceitful appearances in a world of flux.[52] Shakespeare uses the deceptive Protean actor to adumbrate an even broader theme in the culmination of the Duke of Gloucester's soliloquy in *Henry VI, Part III*:

> Why, I can smile, and murder whiles I smile,
> And cry "Content" to that which grieves my heart,
> And wet my cheeks with artificial tears,
> And frame my face to all occasions.
> I'll drown more sailors than the mermaid shall;
> I'll slay more gazers than the basilisk;
> I'll play the orator as well as Nestor,

Deceive more slyly than Ulysses could,
And, like a Sinon, take another Troy.
I can add colors to the Chameleon,
Change shapes with Proteus for advantages,
And set the murderous Machiavel to school.

[III.ii.182−93][53]

All of which, as Richard III, he accomplishes. There is no need to dwell upon Gloucester-Richard's Protean abilities as an actor or upon the role his own shape and deformity play in the motivation for his various roles. We might only note that here Proteus the actor shares billing with Sinon and Machiavel, an association which foreshadows the uncivil powers of Proteus—of Proteus as he was in Pope—the poisoner of the body politic.

This hint of the actor as lawbreaker points to Ben Jonson and *Volpone*, where we are also introduced to Proteus' lustful qualities. Deception and lust are linked. Proteus breaks civil laws because he violates natural or sexual ones.

Volpone is a play permeated by the spirit of Proteus. Here, as Pope has it, the monstrous shapes of Protean master and man truly amaze the town. The satiric thrust partially derives from the fact that Volpone, concerned because

I have no wife, no parent, child, allie,
To give my substance to.

[I.i.73−74][54]

has no real substance at all, only forms. But while he is the master of all shapes in this world-as-bestiary, the real Protean genius is Mosca. He is able to deceive even Volpone for a time, and his ability to change shapes is finally unattached to considerations of money or sex or even power. It is the sheer disinterested joy of the artist, employing his native talent with superb skill.

But your fine, elegant rascall, that can rise,
And stoope (almost together) like an arrow;
Shoot through the aire, as nimbly as a starre;
Turne short, as doth a swallow; and be here,

> And there, and here, and yonder, all at once;
> Present to any humour, all occasion;
> And change a visor, swifter, than a thought!
> This is the creature, had the art borne with him;
> Toiles not to learne it, but doth practise it
> Out of most excellent nature.
>
> [III.i.23–32]

Here in Mosca's cold, and later Volpone's much warmer, reveling, we come to the core of the play where, as Alvin Kernan has indicated, the idea of acting is not only allied with deception but also—as it was in Vives, for instance—with man's unlimited potential. Jonson's irony, of course, depends upon our recognition that here the "art" inherent in "most excellent nature" creates only the unnatural and finally ranges man among the beasts and not the angels.[55]

It is Volpone who explicitly mentions Proteus when he tells Celia that before

> I would have left my practice, for thy love,
> In varying figures, I would have contended
> With the blue PROTEUS.
>
> [III.vii.151–53]

He then offers to contend on the spot. In his seduction of Celia, he promises the delicacies of all the world and the entertainment of his household—all while

> We, in changed shapes, act OVIDS Tales,
> Thou, like EUROPA now, and I like JOVE,
> Then I like MARS, and thou like ERYCINE,
> So, of the rest, till we have quite run through
> And weary'd all the fables of the gods.
>
> [III.vii.221–25]

He expatiates on "more moderne formes" (226) and after a brave catalog of Celia's transformations, he promises: "And I will meet thee, in as many shapes" (233). The language of Proteus limns the limits of man's desires and reveals the terrible emptiness of Volpone, whose appetite can never be satisfied. His marvelous words are impotent, though he claims he is not (260–61). Volpone, who will never again soar so high, ends finally bereft of any "substance" (V.xii. 119) he had left and "crampt with irons" (123) in the hospital of the *Incurabili*—a Proteus at last tied down by the state to become in truth what he had feigned.

Again Proteus the actor or deceiver has threatened the orderly processes of the human community. However in Volpone, he has added a new role to his repertoire, that of a figure of powerful sexual lust. There is some classical precedent for this role of libidinous Proteus. For besides the classical sources for Volpone's boast to weary all the fables of the gods, Lucian in *On Sacrifices* compares amorous Zeus, who inspired all the fables, specifically with Proteus.[56] Certainly, if like Burton one associated Proteus with melancholy, Aristotle's comment in the *Problems* (953b) that "the melancholic are usually lustful" would have been provocative. So would Protean Silenus' promise in Virgil's *Eclogue* VI (25–26) to sing a song for the shepherds but to give the nymph Aegle another kind of reward. These various hints as well as Marlowe's lines in *Hero and Leander* describing the carvings on Venus' temple all underline Volpone's Protean sexuality:

> Wherein was Proteus carv'd, and o'rehead
> A livelie vine of greene sea agget spread . . .
> There might you see the gods in sundrie shapes,
> Committing headdie ryots, incest, rapes.
>
> [I. 137–38, 143–44][57]

Proteus also had a well-established reputation for lust and passion among other Renaissance writers. Boccaccio said Proteus' various forms signified the passions which torment men; Alciati cited Clement of Alexandria who compares Proteus "ad cupiditatem animi humani in varias sese mutantem formas" ("to man's desires which take on various forms"); and Erasmus in his vastly popular *Enchiridion*, in a passage I referred to at the outset, says that when "vehementibus perturbationibus aestuat animus" ("your mind is agitated by violent emotions") you must use every resource to bind this Proteus with chains:

> Quid autem tam Proteus, quam adfectus & cupiditates stultorum, quae cum eas nunc in belluinam libidinem, nunc in iram ferinam, nunc in venenatam invidiam, nunc in alia atque alia vitiorum portenta trahunt.

> What is more like Proteus than the passions and lusts of fools, when they bring on first bestial desire, then wild rage, poisoned jealousy, and then only more and more monstrosities of vice.[58]

Finally, Proteus' reputation for sinister sexuality was only confirmed through his association with a figure like Circe. And if we wonder why Erasmus, in his *Adagia*, would link Proteus and Vertumnus, the reason is manifest when we read in Ovid (*Metamorphoses*, XIV.628–771) of how Vertumnus seduced Pomona by assuming a disguise. Cartari will even describe Vertumnus as a figure for changeable human thought—a common designation for Proteus.[59]

The version of lustful Proteus is linked to the greater role of Proteus lawbreaker. This tradition, already mentioned in Shakespeare's *Richard III*, in *Volpone*, and *The Dunciad*, sees Proteus as uncivil, the violator of social and communal norms and well-being. In *Orlando Furioso*, Ariosto will use both the smaller and the larger roles. There the sea god's lust explicitly ruins a society.

As usual with Ariosto, the episode begins in a previous episode, and one must go back to Angelica to understand Proteus. In Canto VIII, stanzas 29ff., she is fleeing from Europe, and an old hermit, who has befriended her for reasons of his own, despairs of keeping pace. So he enchants her horse which, after a detour in the sea, brings her back to the hermit amid rocks and fearsome caves (37). The old man assaults her and she, "sdegnosetta" ("somewhat supercilious"), pushes him over with one hand, not forgetting to blush her famous blush (47). The resourceful hermit then drugs her by spraying a potion in her eyes, and she is his. But, as stanzas 49 and 50 make wickedly clear, all to no avail. Thus far we have burlesque in the assaults of the old magician, who is impotent; next comes the serious story of Proteus, who is not.[60]

Ariosto now digresses to tell the ancient history of the inhabitants of Ebuda (one of the Hebrides) and their beautiful princess who one day on the beach was raped by Proteus (52). The rape is narrated swiftly and casually in two lines, as if this were standard behavior for Proteus, while the murder of the princess and her child by the men of her enraged and brutal father occupies a stanza. The language now becomes crucial:

> Proteo marin, che pasce il fiero armento
> Di Nettuno che l'onda tutta regge,
> Sente de la sua donna aspro tormento
> E per grand'ira, rompe ordine e legge;
> Sí che a mandare in terra non è lento
> L'orche e le foche, e tutto il marin gregge,
> Che distruggon non sol pecore e buoi,
> Ma ville e borghi, e li cultori suoi:
>
> [54]

> E spesso vanno alle città murate,
> E d'ogn'intorno lor mettono assedio.
> Notte e dí stanno le persone armate,
> Con gran timore, e dispiacevol tedio;
> Tutte hanno le campagne abbandonate.
>
> [55]

Proteus, the sea god who pastures the fierce herds of Neptune, ruler of the ocean, heard the bitter torment of his lady and, in a wild rage, broke all bounds and limits; so that he did not hesitate to send ashore his orcs and seals, and all his ocean flock, to ravage not only the sheep and cattle, but farms and villages, and those who toiled there:

And often they came to fortified cities and laid seige to them on all sides. Night and day the townspeople stand guard, in great fear and tiresome monotony. All the fields lay abandoned.

From Proteus' rape comes the slaughter of a girl by her father, and after that follow violations of other laws: first, the "ordine e legge" of nature governing the habitat and behavior of the sea creatures, and second, the assault of nature on nature—as the sea creatures attack the oxen and sheep—and then nature on the farms and their "cultori" and finally on the walled cities. We have worked up the scale of being and inland to the centers of civilization.

From the sexual lawlessness and civil discord comes, inevitably, more of the same. The oracle consulted by the islanders advises offering girls to Proteus in appeasement for the dead princess (56), and as these human sacrifices are bound to a rock, the monstrous orc consumes them (57). On Ebuda, this is the "empia legge antica" ("pitiless, ancient law" 58)—the new law which long ago resulted from the rupture of the old. Thus, Angelica—"in braccio al santo padre" ("in the arms of the venerable father" 61)—is found by a party searching for new victims, for the people have long since become obsessed and depraved, "sì barbare . . . e sì villane" ("so barbarous . . . and so base" 62). And after Angelica is exposed (67) and the story resumed when Ruggiero comes to her rescue (X.93), the barbarism and incivility of the islanders is continually stressed (X.93, 95). This whole episode culminates in Canto XI when Orlando finally kills the orc and the sea runs with blood while all the sea creatures lament terribly (44–45). The people, terrified of Proteus and his "ira insana" (46), assault rather than welcome their benefactor, and Orlando is forced to kill a number of the "gente pazza" (50). Finally the human community which decayed within so long ago is destroyed without as a party of Irish land and kill all the islanders and raze their cities' walls. In the meantime, Orlando, defender of another city, Paris, walks away.

Throughout the episodes involving Proteus and Ebuda, Ariosto's sense of the marvelous never falters. But noticeably absent is his habitual ironic preoccupation with the discrepancy between illusion and reality, perhaps because the incidents involving Proteus are part of a more somber theme in the poem, the insanity which is caused by love and, finally, the insanity which is love. This madness, afflicting the islanders and Proteus in different forms, finally will overwhelm Orlando himself, and in all cases Angelica, or, as in Canto VIII, her surrogate the princess, is the cause. However, we might also suggest that the Proteus episodes lack Ariosto's customary irony because that is what the episodes are about: they deal with that loss of balance, of perspective, of proportion—irony in its largest sense—without which men are doomed and which men seemed forever doomed to lack. "Grand' ira" (VIII.54), "ira insana" (XI.46), says the poet of Proteus, for Proteus, casual, brutal, and assured, is our key to the incipient frenzy and overmastering destructive power in us all. While as a lesson teaching what those forces can do, the sexual barbarism of Proteus has caused the death of a city.[61]

At this point, it is fair to say that the incivility of Proteus, Proteus as lawbreaker, has been implicit in all the darker hues on all the spectra—whether in Proteus as poet (as in *The Dunciad*) or as actor (as in *Volpone*) or as sinister rapist (as in the *Orlando Furioso*). As we have come to expect, however, a given version of Proteus always implies its opposite, and there is also the civic Proteus, the figure of concord, not discord, the maker of civilization, not death and destruction. More than once we have mentioned Vives' *Fabula*, deriving from Pico's *Oratio*, where Protean man was a builder of cities, a giver of laws, "in every way a political and social being."[62] The most striking versions of the civic Proteus in the Renaissance, however, are found in its most influential mythographer and its greatest poet. Differing and unrelated as these versions are, they demonstrate that Comes and Shakespeare could see the Proteus figure as containing all and the Protean spirit as a force for good.

In his long account of Proteus, Comes saw him as the original principle of all things; as a wise man and author of works on natural philosophy; as a *vates* and as one who practiced magic arts (these two are distinguished); as a man whose words could move the souls of men; and finally as the "populorum pastores," the type of the prince who considered the health as well as the comfort of his people.

I think, says Comes finally, that Proteus is a wise man *(virum prudentem)* who draws men into concord and warm friendship and soothes souls, who heals the differences arising among them and teaches them to adapt to the human condition. For, Comes contin-

ues, who does not know there is no greater thing, "vel in adminis-
tratione ciuitatum, vel quotidiana consuetudine" ("whether in the
administration of states, or in daily relations"), than to accommodate
the spirit to changing situations and to changes in human affairs?

> Oportet igitur virum prudentem, quoniam non omnes ijsdem studiis
> delectanur aut capiuntur, per varias formas se in hominum amicitiam
> ingerere, ac variis uti rationibus in civitatum administrationibus,
> quoniam alij eventus clementiam, alii severitatem iudicis requirunt.

> Since not everyone enjoys or involves himself in the same pursuits, it is
> fitting that the wise man promote himself in various capacities within
> human society, and that he make use of various systems of civil
> administration, seeing as some situations require a judge's clemency,
> while others demand stringency on his part.

Thus the Renaissance principle of tolerance, of amending oneself to
the necessities of life, of adapting oneself to one's sense of the
contingencies in things, underlies the proper government of the city
of man. And Proteus, whose various forms signify the wise man's
ability to influence men for the good, is a proper figure for this
principle of flexible civility.

But the fable does not only pertain to friendship and civil administration, Comes says. Above all it relates "ad universam humanae vitae
rationem" ("to the universal principle of human life"), which consists
neither in gorging oneself nor in living austerely. Rather the proper
time for things must be recognized ("sed utriusque rei tempora sunt
cognoscenda"). Comes concludes that to him the fable means no more
than what the oracle said:

> Ne quid nimis: cum omnis omnium rerum salus & constantia in
> mediocritate, moderationeque sit collocata,

Nothing in excess, for the health and constancy of all things consists
of mediocrity and moderation in all things: The ethical life underlies
the civic life, as in a powerful exordium to his readers Comes
transmits the essentials of the humanistic wisdom drawn from the
ancients. And Proteus, the man whose friendship, prudence, and

civic sense are figured by his ability to adapt to the demands of life and the needs of man, is the symbol for it all.[63]

Our final consideration of Proteus will be as one of the two main characters in Shakespeare's *The Two Gentlemen of Verona*. Indeed, we may ask why Shakespeare chose the name at all, for it appears in none of the play's sources.[64] The usual answer—that this is a comedy of true and false friendship and love where Valentine figures faithfulness and Proteus, inconstancy—is not adequate, for it ignores both the full possibilities in the name and Shakespeare's exploitation of them. In *Two Gentlemen of Verona*, Proteus plays all the roles we have examined, and Shakespeare extends the spirit of Proteus in order to supersede the figure of Proteus. At least, the figure is superseded as it contains sinister elements. Finally, even the purged figure is redeemed by the spirit.

In the play's Protean world, where love has "metamorphos'd" both Proteus and Valentine (I.i.66, II.i.32) and "deform'd" Valentine's Silvia (II.i.70), Proteus easily plays all his traditional roles. The "subtile, perju'd, false, disloyal man," as Silvia calls him in IV.ii.95, is an actor or deceiver throughout. He is also an artist in III.ii.51–87, where he is compared to a weaver and a sculptor, and where he acts, on Sir Thurio's behalf, as a poet and a stage director. As before he was a figure for language, here in the balcony scene he is allied with the instability of music (IV.ii.54–72). And he is still the traditional manipulator of language in IV.ii.120–34 as he, Silvia, and Julia (disguised as a boy—another form of deformation) talk about the ambiguities of illusion and reality, "shadow" and "substance," their puns demonstrating and embodying those ambiguities. Finally, Proteus is throughout a corrupter and a would-be seducer; he is even willing, as he was in Ariosto, Spenser, and Jonson, to be a rapist (V.iv.55–58). His reference to his own "augury" in IV.iv.73 even recalls the traditional role as Proteus, *vates*.

In Act V, the banished Valentine is in a wood outside Milan, the chief of a band of outlaws. He is worried that his men "make their wills their law" and that it is difficult "to keep them from uncivil outrages" (iv. 14, 17). When he sees Proteus assault Silvia, who has come to find him, Valentine cries, "Ruffian! let go that rude, uncivil touch" (60) and the deeper issue of law and lawlessness—civility in its widest sense—begins to develop. After sharply rebuking Proteus, Valentine forgives him and then—gives him Silvia (77–83). This episode, a scandal to commentators, was once adduced as proof Shakespeare was not the only begetter of *Two Gentlemen of Verona*[65] and is usually justified by the conventions of male friendship. But it seems clear that what is at work here is simply the spirit of Proteus; for now the play begins to supersede the figure while developing the spirit—the spirit of Proteus in Comes's terms of concord and amendment.

Men are first reconciled with themselves: Julia reveals her true nature and identity; Proteus seemingly sees his falsity (108–12). Men are then reconciled with each other, as Valentine, embodying the spirit of adaptability, friendship, and healing, invites Proteus and Julia: "Come, come, a hand from either. . . . 'Twere pity two such friends should be long foes" (116–18). "Bear witness, heaven, I have my wish forever" (119), says Proteus, and by implying constancy ceases to be Proteus. He never speaks again.

The Protean spirit, however, continues to work its good. Sir Thurio now reverses himself and renounces his claim to Silvia, thus causing the Duke to turn on him, a conversion which reconciles the Duke with Valentine, in whom he recognizes "unrivall'd merit" (144). And now the Protean spirit of lawgiving completely surpasses lawbreaking, as Valentine asks for his outlaws the same recognition of inner worth he has received.

> Forgive them what they have committed here
> And let them be recall'd from their exile.
> They are reformed, civil, full of good.
>
> [154–56]

The deformations of Proteus and Protean love are now "reformed" on the widest scale by the Protean spirit embodied in Valentine. Men find themselves and each other, the outlaws are included in the new law, the forest is reconciled with the city, and "civil" restoration is effected within and without.

Nothing is beyond the healing spirit. "Come Proteus," says Valentine,

> 'Tis your penance but to hear
> The story of your loves discovered.
> That done, our day of marriage shall be yours;
> One feast, one house, one mutual happiness.

[170–73]

Valentine will "discover" or reveal the final shape of Proteus himself, and with that reformation the civilizing spirit will have reclaimed the purged figure of this society's greatest outlaw. In the rituals of marriage and feast, those ceremonies of social harmony, and in the house, very symbol of the city, the Protean spirit of reconciliation will reside. In drawing the spirit of concord from the figure of discord, the play has reversed itself and is revealed as an example of what it is about.

Mutability, lawlessness, baseness, constancy, civility, gentility: in addition to his traditional roles, Proteus as figure and spirit has signified them all. There is no more inclusive vision of the versions of Proteus in the Renaissance, no clearer depiction of his dangers and redeeming possibilities.

In the last decade of the sixteenth century, those redeeming possibilities—the spirit of Proteus to unite and to civilize—extended beyond the romantic comedy of Shakespeare. In *The Faerie Queene*, when Medway relents and will marry Thames,

> both agreed that this their bridale feast
> Should for the gods in Proteus house be made.

[IV.xi.9]

And so they go, in grand and spacious order, all the gods and waters great and small. The bride, with flowers scattered in her hair, upon her head "A chaplet of sundry flowers . . . wore" (76), while he, "a coronet . . . In which were many towres and castels set" (27), a crown like Cybele's, symbol of the city, Troynovant. This great myth of the most ceremonious of all Renaissance poets marries all—male and female, art and nature, the city and the garden worlds—through the pageant in Proteus' house. And perhaps after all the versions, this should be the final one, the last thought to have of Proteus: like the Renaissance poet, entertaining the very stuff of creation, presiding over the most civilizing of ceremonies, while participating in and controlling a world of ceaseless change.

Notes

Chapter 1: The Forms of Epic

1   *The Poet and His Faith* (Chicago: University of Chicago Press, 1965), p. 21.

Chapter 2: Hippolytus among the Exiles

I wish to acknowledge the help of Mr. Stephen Cushman, without whose scholarship and diligence this essay could not have been prepared for publication. Rarely have I had such a congenial collaborator.

1   *Francisci Petrarcae Epistolae De Rebus Familiaribus Et Variae,* ed. Giuseppe Fracassetti (Florence: Typis Felicis Le Monnier, 1859), I:2; Morris Bishop, trans., *Letters From Petrarch* (Bloomington: Indiana University Press, 1966), p. 7.

2   Fracassetti, *Epistolae,* I:18; Bishop, *Letters,* pp. 18−19.

3   *Epistole di Francesco Petrarca,* ed. Ugo Dotti, U.T.E.T., 4 vols. (Turin, 1978) 2: 888; Bishop, *Letters,* p. 12.

4   On this theme in later Renaissance epics, see chapter 3 below, "Headlong Horses, Headless Horsemen."

5   For a later version of this idea as located in lost children and foundlings, see chapter 5 below, "Primitivism and the Process of Civility in Spenser's *Faerie Queene.*"

6   Fracassetti, *Epistolae,* I:90; Francesco Petrarca, *Rerum familiarium libri I–VIII,* trans. Aldo S. Bernardo (Albany: State University of New York Press, 1975), p. 71.

7   Fracassetti, *Epistolae,* I:90−91; Bernardo, *Rerum familiarium,* pp. 71−72.

8   Fracassetti, *Epistolae* (1863), III:80; my translation.

9   *The Renaissance Sense of the Past* (London: Edward Arnold, 1969), p. 21.

10 For these matters the basic text is Wallace Ferguson, *The Renaissance in Historical Thought: Five Centuries of Interpretation* (Cambridge: Harvard University Press, 1948).

11 Fracassetti, *Epistolae,* III:279; Mario Cosenza, trans., *Petrarch's Letters to Classical*

Authors (Chicago: University of Chicago Press, 1910), p. 88. Where I have used Cosenza's translation, I have somewhat modernized his diction.

12 Fracassetti, *Epistolae,* III:278; Cosenza, *Petrarch's Letters,* p. 84.

13 Fracassetti, *Epistolae,* III:278; Cosenza, *Petrarch's Letters,* pp. 84–85.

14 Text and translation from *Virgil,* ed. H. R. Fairclough, Loeb Classical Library, 2 vols., rev. ed. (Cambridge: Harvard University Press, 1969, 1974). Although I have used Fairclough's translation, I have modernized his diction and arranged the prose in verse form.

15 On Virbius, particularly in Dante, see Marguerite Mills Chiarenza, "Hippolytus' Exile: *Paradiso* XVII, vv. 46–48," *Dante Studies* 84 (1966), 65–68.

16 On the tradition of the healer in the Christian Middle Ages, see Rudolph Arbesmann, "The Concept of 'Christus Medicus' in St. Augustine," *Traditio* 10 (1954), 1–28.

17 Fracassetti, *Epistolae,* III:280; Cosenza, *Petrarch's Letters,* p. 89.

18 Fracassetti, *Epistolae,* III:278; Cosenza, *Petrarch's Letters,* p. 85.

19 Remigio Sabbadini, *Le Scoperte dei codici latini e greci ne' secoli, XIV e XV,* rev. and ed. Eugenio Garin (Florence: Sansoni, 1967), I:78. For an older account, see J. E. Sandys, *A History of Classical Scholarship* (Cambridge: Cambridge University Press, 1908), II:27. For further bibliography on Poggio's four expeditions, see the excellent account of Rudolf Pfeiffer, *History of Classical Scholarship from 1300 to 1850* (Oxford: Oxford University Press, Clarendon Press, 1976), pp. 31–34.

20 *Epistolarum familiarium libri VIII,* ed. Antonio Moreto and Girolamo Squarciafico (Venice: Damianus de Gorgonzola and Petrus de Quarengis, 1495), Bk. IV, ltr. 5, n.p.; Phyllis Gordan, trans., *Two Renaissance Book Hunters* (New York: Columbia University Press, 1974), p. 191. I cite the Latin text of 1495 with all abbreviations expanded.

21 Moreto and Squarciafico, *Epistolarum,* n. p.; Gordan, *Book Hunters,* p. 192.

22 Moreto and Squarciafico, *Epistolarum,* n. p.; Gordan, *Book Hunters,* p. 192.

23 *Poggii Epistolae,* ed. Thomas de Tonellis (Florence: Typis L. Marchini, 1832), Bk. I, ltr. 5, vol. 1, p. 26; reprinted in *Poggii Opera Omnia,* ed. Riccardo Fubini (Turin: Bottega d'Erasmo, 1964), vol. 3; Gordan, *Book Hunters,* p. 193.

24 de Tonellis, *Epistolae,* I:27; Cosenza, *Petrarch's Letters,* p. 92.

25 de Tonellis, *Epistolae,* I:27; Gordan, *Book Hunters,* p. 194.

26 Fairclough, *Virgil.*

27 Fairclough, *Virgil.*

28 de Tonellis, *Epistolae,* I:27; Gordan, *Book Hunters,* p. 194.

29 de Tonellis, *Epistolae,* I:27–28; Gordan, *Book Hunters,* p. 194.

30 *Francisci Barbari et aliorum ad ipsum Epistolae,* ed. A. M. Quirini (Brescia: Joannes-Maria Rizzardi, 1743), p. 2; Gordan, *Book Hunters,* p. 196.

31 Quirini, *Epistolae,* p. 2; Gordan, *Book Hunters,* pp. 196–97.

32 Quirini, *Epistolae,* p. 2; Gordan, *Book Hunters,* p. 197.

33 Quirini, *Epistolae,* pp. 2–3; Gordan, *Book Hunters,* p. 197.

34 Quirini, *Epistolae,* p. 3; Gordan, *Book Hunters,* p. 198.

35 *Genealogia Deorum Gentilium* (Venice: Wendelin von Speyer, 1472), n. p.; Charles Osgood, trans., *Boccaccio on Poetry,* 2nd ed. (New York: Bobbs-Merrill, 1956), pp. 5–6. I cite the Latin text of 1472 with abbreviations expanded.

36 *Genealogia*, n. p.; Osgood, *Boccaccio*, p. 6.
37 *Genealogia*, n. p.; Osgood, *Boccaccio*, p. 10.
38 *Genealogia*, n. p.; Osgood, *Boccaccio*, pp. 10–11.
39 *Genealogia*, n. p.; Osgood, *Boccaccio*, p. 11.
40 *Genealogia*, n. p.; Osgood, *Boccaccio*, p. 12.
41 *Genealogia*, n. p.; Osgood, *Boccaccio*, p. 13.
42 See Chiarenza, "Hippolytus' Exile," pp. 65–66.

Chapter 3: *The Chivalric Epics of Pulci, Boiardo, and Ariosto*

1 Text and translation from *Virgil*, ed. H. R. Fairclough, Loeb Classical Library, 2 vols., rev. ed. (London and Cambridge, Mass., 1965).

2 In Greek writing, the predominant images for horses out of control involve horses and chariots. Hippolytus, whose name means "loosened" or "liberated" horse, is the master image for the tragic end to unruly passions. For the ethical and erotic impulses of man, there is Plato's image of the two winged horses of the soul, the one "noble and good, and of good stock," the other quite the opposite (*Phaedrus*, 246b), and their charioteer (253c, 254a). Representations of *riding* are rare in Greek art and literature before 700 B.C.—Homer speaks of riding only twice, and then in similes (*Iliad* 15.679, *Odyssey* 5.371), though he does show chariot horses ridden under extraordinary circumstances (*Iliad* 10.512 f). See J. K. Anderson, *Ancient Greek Horsemanship* (University of California Press, 1961), p. 10. Because ancient riders, Greek and Roman, had no stirrups, there are instances mentioned by historians of riders dying as a result of their inability to control their horses—Tacitus, *Agricola* 37.6; Plutarch, *Artaxerxes* 21 (Anderson, pp. 76–77). On the stirrup and its importance, especially to chivalry, see Lynn White, Jr., *Medieval Technology and Social Change* (Oxford University Press, 1962), pp. 1–38.

3 The ancients seemed to emphasize different parts of the centaur: Nessus, who would have raped Deianira, is the lower part; Chiron, already remembered in the *Iliad* (4.219) for his healing arts, is the upper, human part.

4 Text from *The Theological Tracts*, ed. H. F. Stewart and E. K. Rand, Loeb Classical Library (Cambridge, Mass. and London, 1918); I have used the translation in the Library of Liberal Arts of Richard Green (Indianapolis and New York, 1962).

5 I use the two-volume edition of G. Busnelli and G. Vandelli in the series *Opere di Dante*, ed. M. Barbi (Florence, 1934). On temperance, and spurring and curbing a horse (and the *Aeneid*), see also *Convivio* IV.26.5–11. Henceforth, all translations are mine unless otherwise noted.

6 See *Convivio* vol. 2, p. 101 for other versions of the image and explications.

7 Text from *La Divina Commedia*, ed. C. H. Grandgent, rev. C. S. Singleton (Cambridge, Mass.: Harvard University Press, 1972). Translation from *The Divine Comedy*, trans. and ed. T. G. Bergin (New York: Crofts Classics, 1955).

8 Luigi Pulci (1432–84). *Morgante* begun in 1461; Cantos I–XXIII.47 printed in 1478; Cantos XVIII.112–XIX.155 (Margutte episode) printed separately, 1480–81. Both publications were lost; other versions printed in 1481 and 1482, while Pulci was also working on a second poem, finished after 25 March 1482; the two poems published together as one, 7 February 1483. Text used is *Morgante*, ed.

F. Ageno, *Letteratura Italiana, Storia e Testi* 17 (Milan-Naples, 1955). Translations mine. Ageno has a good bibliography, pp. xxviii–xxx; I would only add, in English, L. Einstein, *Luigi Pulci and The Morgante Maggiore, Litteraturhistorische Forschungen,* vol. 22 (Berlin, 1902), and G. Grillo, *Two Aspects of Chivalry, Pulci and Boiardo* (Boston, 1942), though this last is less helpful. For Pulci's cultural milieu and relevant bibliography, see E. A. Lebano, "Luigi Pulci and Late Fifteenth-Century Humanism in Florence," *Renaissance Quarterly* 27 (1974):489–98. For a survey of the Italian epic including Pulci, Boiardo, and Ariosto, see the introduction to *Ludovico Ariosto Orlando Furioso,* trans. W. S. Rose, ed. S. A. Baker and A. B. Giamatti, Library of Literature (New York, Indianapolis, 1968); also, a survey of translations of these poets and others by K. J. Atchity, "Renaissance Epics in English," *Italica* 50, no. 3 (1973):435–39. Also see below, nn. 15 and 18.

9   The contrast between Jehoshaphat (Joel 3:2), the scene of the resurrection of the dead (also *Morgante* I.6; III.43), and Roncesvalles, the "dolente valle" ("sorrowful valley"), "Caïna d'inferno" ("Caïna of Hell"), full of dead at XXVII.201, is another instance of the dialectic, of Pulci's constant desire to believe in something better and his awareness of decay beneath everything.

10   Ageno cites a codex where *mortito* is defined as being made "con un capo di porco e dodici piedi di castrone cotti nel vino rosso con coccole di mortine, garofani, cannella e pepe" ("with the head of a pig and twelve feet of a gelding cooked in red wine with myrtle berries, clove, cinnamon, and pepper"), *Morgante,* VII.56, p. 168. The animal parts in red wine are a ghastly analogue to the carnage of war. And was there not a punning echo of the *mortito* in the *cavallo,* who after Rinaldo struck him, fell "come e' fussi tramortito"? (XIII.65).

11   Warfare—and thus, in this world—life, as *gioco*: III.49, XIII.64, XIX.37, 112, XX.68, XXI.74, XXII.138, 170, XXVII.27; for references to "fare il gioco netto," see XI.37, XIII.62, XVII.12, 64, XXVI.151, XXVIII.21.

12   Desiderius Erasmus, *The Praise of Folly,* trans. H. Hudson (Princeton, 1941), p. 38. On play, see J. Huizinga's classic *Homo Ludens* (Boston, 1950), especially pp. 180–82.

13   *El Ingenioso Hidalgo Don Quixote de la Mancha,* ed. F. Rodríguez Marín (new ed., Madrid, 1948), 5, 174.

14   On Arnaldo, see XXV.115, XXVIII.26.

15   Matteo Maria Boiardo (1441–94). *Orlando Innamorato,* begun in the 1460s; Books I (29 cantos) and II (31 cantos) published together in 1483; Book III (9 cantos) published separately in 1495; all three books published together first in 1495. Text used: *Orlando Innamorato, Amorum Libri,* ed. A. Scaglione, Classici Italiani, 2 vols. (Turin, 1963). Translations mine. Scaglione has a useful bibliography in 1.37–41. Now there are the papers of the Boiardo Congress, Scandiano, Reggio-Emilia, 1969, in *Il Boiardo e la critica contemporanea,* ed. G. Anceschi (Florence, 1970). Criticism in English: Sir Antonio Panizzi published, with Italian text and English notes, Boiardo's *Orlando Innamorato* (4 vols.) and Ariosto's *Orlando Furioso* (4 vols.), with an introductory volume on romantic narrative (London, 1830–34); J. A. Symonds, *Renaissance in Italy, Italian Literature,* 2 vols. (London, 1881),

now in Capricorn Books (New York, 1964), 1:371–432, on "Pulci and Boiardo"; Vernon Lee [Violet Paget], *Euphorion: Being Studies of the Antique and Mediaeval in the Renaissance*, 2 vols. (London, 1884), discusses Boiardo in each volume; E. W. Edwards, *The Orlando Furioso and its Predecessor* (Cambridge, 1924). Of recent criticism in English, there is a fine chapter in R. Durling, *The Figure of the Poet in Renaissance Epic* (Cambridge, Mass.: Harvard University Press, 1965), and a study by A. Di Tommaso, *Structure and Ideology in Boiardo's Orlando Innamorato*, University of North Carolina Studies in Romance Languages and Literatures, vol. 23 (Chapel Hill, 1972). See also n. 8 above and n. 18 below for relevant items.

16 See the preparation for this event, at II.xxviii.21, when the court goes to battle, substituting for *danze* (dances) a cacophony of men, instruments, and dogs: "Par che 'l cel cada e 'l mondo abbia a finire" ("It seems that the heavens fall and the world comes to an end").

17 Compare a similar stanza on his own art by Pulci, *Morgante* XXVIII.140.

18 Ludovico Ariosto (1474–1533). *Orlando Furioso* was begun by 1509 and published in forty cantos, 1516; 2d rev. ed., forty cantos, 1521; 3d ed., forty-six cantos, 1532. Text used: *Orlando Furioso*, ed. L. Caretti, La Letteratura Italiana, Storia e Testi 19 (Milan-Naples, 1954); notes to *Orlando Furioso* in vol. 2, *Opere Minori*, ed. C. Segre. Translations are from the W. S. Rose translation, ed. Baker and Giamatti, with my emendations in brackets. I have not adopted Rose's spelling of proper names. There is a vast literature on Ariosto; the best review of Ariosto's critical "fortune" and a listing of basic bibliographies and monographs is in Mario Puppo, *Manuale critico-bibliografico per lo studio della letteratura italiana*, 5th rev. ed. (Turin, 1964), pp. 243–52; see also the entry "Ludovico Ariosto" by N. Sapegno in *Dizionario Biografico degli Italiani* (Rome, 1962), 4.172–88. For criticism in English, see the bibliography in the Rose translation, pp. xlv–xlvi. Two full-length studies of Ariosto and his poem in English are: Robert Griffin, *Ludovico Ariosto*, Twayne World Authors Series (New York: Twayne Publishers, 1974) and C. P. Brand, *Ludovico Ariosto: Preface to the Orlando Furioso* (Edinburgh: Edinburgh University Press, 1974). Also see above, nn. 8 and 15 for relevant items.

19 *Istoria* (118; 120) is also the poem's word for itself—see XIII.80 or XXIII.136—as the analogy between Orlando's predicament and the reader's is maintained throughout.

20 Earlier occurrences of *senno* at IV.65 and XXVII.8 contribute to the meaning of sensible, reasonable, and ethical behavior that the word acquires in the poem.

21 For *sereno*, see the serene air (IV.43), sky (XXVII.8), faces of God (XVII.6), Christians (XLIII.199), or serene eyes obscured (I.79; XI.64)—all images of the integrated ideal we must strive for. This particular pattern of imagery has an important history, and implications, in the Renaissance epic: see chapter 4 below, "Spenser: From Magic to Miracle."

Chapter 4: Spenser

1 *Hurd's Letters on Chivalry and Romance with the Third Elizabethan Dialogue*, ed. Edith J. Morley (London: H. Frowde, 1911), pp. 113, 136, 153.

2   The gesture itself is by no means confined to the Renaissance. The reader will have
     already recalled the moment in *Iliad* VI when Astyanax screams at the sight of
     Hector's menacing plumage: "Then his beloved father laughed out, and his
     honoured mother, / And at once glorious Hector lifted from his head the hel-
     met / And laid it in all its shining upon the ground" (471-73); in Book XXII,
     Andromache sees Hector dragged before the city; she "threw from her head the
     shining gear that ordered her headdress, / the diadem and the cap, and the hold-
     ing band woven together, / and the circlet which Aphrodite the golden once had
     given her" (468-70, Richmond Lattimore translation). The single gesture unites
     the family; the revelation of fatherhood, which soothes the son, is paralleled by the
     mother's uncovering, which underscores her inadequacy to confer identity and
     prefaces her poignant lament for the fate of her fatherless boy. The mutual needs of
     fathers and sons are at the heart of the poem. Nor should we forget the Archangel
     Michael, emissary of another Father, who comes to Adam and Eve: "His starry
     Helm unbuckl'd show'd him prime / In Manhood where Youth ended" (*Paradise
     Lost* XI.245-46). The chivalric romance gives Milton this helmet and the face
     whose perfection resides in its balance of antithetical qualities.

3   Ludovico Ariosto, *Orlando Furioso*, ed. Nicola Zingarelli (Milan: Ulrico Hoepli,
     1959); unless otherwise noted, all translations are my own.

4   On a woman's face, and smile, making paradise, see Dante, *Paradiso* XV.34-36;
     Petrarch, *Rime* CCXCII.5-7; parodied, as usual, by Pulci, *Morgante* XV.102 and
     XVI.12.

5   Boiardo, *Orlando Innamorato*, ed. Francesco Foffano, 3 vols. (Milan: UTET, 1944).

6   Text taken from *Dante's Purgatorio*, trans. and commentary by John Sinclair
     (New York: Oxford University Press, 1961); I have arranged as verse a some-
     what revised translation.

7   Luigi Pulci, *Morgante,* ed. Franca Ageno (Milan and Naples: Riccardo Ric-
     ciardi, 1955).

8   *Virgil,* ed. and trans. H. R. Fairclough, Loeb Classical Library, rev. ed. (London
     and Cambridge, Mass., 1935); text used as basis of my translation.

9   An interesting example of the greater flexibility of a "medieval" as opposed to a
     Renaissance poet in adapting material from powerful literary models occurs in
     the treatments by Chaucer and Boccaccio of the revelations of Emilia to the
     imprisoned Palemon and Arcite. In *Teseida* III.8-14, Emilia's appearance in the
     garden and her effect on the men (Arcita: "Disse fra sè: questa è di paradiso,"
     12) is closely modeled on Matelda's appearance to and colloquy with the pilgrim
     and his guide in Eden, particularly *Purgatorio* XXVIII.37-42, 61-66, 80-81.
     Even Palemon's reference to Venus (stanza 14) seems to derive from Dante's
     reference at XXVIII.64-66. Chaucer, in *The Knight's Tale,* 1033-1122, shows
     much more range in his resourcefulness. The account of Emelye's hair, garland and
     singing as an "angel hevenysshly" (1049-55) follows *Teseida* III.8-11; but
     Palamon's wonderment: "I noot wher she be woman or goddesse, / But Venus is it
     soothly, as I gesse" (1101-02) conflates Boccaccio with *Aeneid* I.327-29—a
     passage Chaucer also exploited in *Troilus and Criseyde* I.425—and brings Virgilian
     revelation into the English tradition independently of Italian romances. "There-

withal on knees doun he fil, / And seyde: 'Venus, if it by thy wil / You in this garden thus to transfigure / Bifore me . . . '" (1103–06), says Palamon who by kneeling and using the language of religious transformation foreshadows Artegall at *Faerie Queene* IV.vi.22 (see below). Text used: *The Works of Geoffrey Chaucer,* ed. F. N. Robinson (Boston: Houghton Mifflin, 1957).

10   Tasso provides the clearest example of this when Tancredi unwittingly wounds mortally his beloved Clorinda, *Gerusalemme Liberata* XII.67–68. What Tancredi sees upon raising her visor is not immediately described: rather the poet emphasizes the effect of the revelation, tragic knowledge for Tancredi, conversion for Clorinda, and only then (st. 69) describes her face.

11   The *voyeur* is privy to the *voyant's* insight (to no avail) when Sansloy snatches away Una's veil at I.vi.4, and his "lustful eye" feeds on her beauty shining "as brightest skye." The rhyme links the two modes of sight as the gesture links the two figures. The final apotheosis of Una occurs when she has her "widow-like sad wimple throwne away" and the "glorious light of her sunshyny face" (I.xii.22–23) picks up the language of I.iii.4—framing Book I by visions of her face. The light of Heaven is also revealed by another veil falling away—the covering on Arthur's shield which falls in the fight with Orgoglio (I.viii.9) and with the Souldan (V.viii.37). The revelations of the "sunlike shield" (V.viii.41) reestablish for the reader the condition of light and knighthood to which all other lights, and knights, aspire.

12   In the proem to Book II, stanza 5, the face of Elizabeth is by the poet "enfold / In couert vele" because of its exceeding brightness; we get versions of its splendor in the face of Belphoebe, a "heauenly pourtrait of bright Angels hew" (II.iii.22—as seen by the *voyeur* Trompart) and in the angel's face "Like Phoebus . . . [which] Diuinely shone" (II.viii.5); while reminding us of the deceptiveness of revelation, there is in Mammon's cave Philotime's face that "wondrous faire did seeme . . . But wrought by art and counterfetted shew" (II.vii.45). We learn to eschew this "counterfetted shew" and, like Arthur, see the "vertue in vaine shew" (II.ix.3), to see, with Arthur, the living and wholesome ideal in art.

13   See also *Amoretti* XIII, XXII, XXVI. Perfection through such a mix of male and female attributes is part of Spenser's, and the Renaissance's, fascination with the Hermaphrodite.

14   Elizabeth is the fixed light for the poet at I, proem 5; images of fixed stars occur at I.ii.1; VII.vi.9; see also *Epithalamium,* lines 285–91 and 409–12. Lodestar hid in clouds, at III.iv.53, and fixed star covered, II.viii.1, both images related to the recurrent figure of the eye of Reason blinded, I.ii.5, II.iv.7, and IV.ii.5, and to instances of the face of Heaven clouded over, II.xii.34 and III.iv.13.

15   Artegall sees in Radigund's face "A miracle of natures grace" (V.v.12) but he must learn what we learned at V.iii.39, when Braggadocchio and the False Florimel were "uncased," or what we saw in the discoveries of the faces of Duessa and Ate (IV.i.17–19), and of Philotime (II.viii.45) and Archimago (I.iii.38): that not all revelations are benign and wholesome. Artegall must learn the hardest lesson, to distinguish. Like Arthur, he must learn when "to doubt his dazeled sight" (II.xi.40). When Arthur and Artegall gaze at each other through upraised visors,

and Artegall, "touched with entire affection, nigh him drew" (V.viii.12), then Britomart's dream at Isis Church (V.vii.14), her view of Artegall in the flesh (IV.vi.26), and in the magic glass (III.ii.24) begin to take shape as Artegall becomes more Arthur's equal, more a strong but tempered lover.

16   The poem ends with a veiled woman, Nature (VII.vii.5–6), as it began with Una veiled (I.i.4); though Nature, who when veiled resembles Venus (IV.x.41), has male traits, like Britomart, and is dazzling, like Gloriana. Like the poem, which is her glass, Nature contains all.

17   Both Rabelais, Prologue to *The First Book,* and Marino, *L'Adone,* I.10, compare their works to the Silenus. Erasmus was mainly responsible for the diffusion of the Silenus figure in the Renaissance; see, for Erasmus and Rabelais, Walter Kaiser, *Praisers of Folly, Erasmus, Rabelais, Shakespeare* (Cambridge, Mass.: Harvard University Press, 1963), especially pp. 55–60, and for the related figures of the chameleon and Proteus, see chapter 7 below, "Proteus Unbound: Some Versions of the Sea God in the Renaissance." In his *Commentary on Psalm* 33, Erasmus connects the two literary figures for truth beneath the surface: "so far I have presented but the shell of the nut, and thus you have only tasted the husk of the barley; I just showed you Silenus. If God deigns to help us, we shall now extract the kernel, expose the fine flour, and expound Silenus"—cited in the valuable study of Peter G. Bietenholz, *History and Biography in the Works of Erasmus of Rotterdam* (Geneva: Droz, 1966), p. 24.

Chapter 5: *Primitivism and Civility in Spenser's* Faerie Queene

1   See Samuel Flagg Bemis, "'America' and 'Americans'," *The Yale Review* 57 (1968):321–36, especially 321–24; Bemis cites John Rastell as the first Englishman to use "America." See also Edward Gaylord Bourne, "The Naming of America," *American Historical Review* 10 (1904):41–51, especially 46–48 on the Spanish resistance to the name "America." See also n. 2 below.

2   OED, s.v. "Americall" and "American." Noah Biggs, *Mataeotechnia Medicinae Praxeos. The Vanity of the Craft of Physick, or, A New Dispensatory . . . With an humble Motion for the Reformation of the UNIVERSITIES and the whole Landscap of PHYSICK, and discovering the Terra Incognita of CHYMISTRIE* (London, 1651). In speaking of the inefficacy of laxatives and purges, Biggs says: "neither do any diseases *respond* or goe a *pilgrimage* to lodge in the *New-found-Land* of *Americall* or *Prestor-John* humours." Para. 124, p. 78.

3   For an excellent discussion of "Civility," see W. Gordon Zeeveld, *The Temper of Shakespeare's Thought* (New Haven, 1974), pp. 185–257; Spenser is discussed, pp. 191–201. Zeeveld touches on all the Elizabethan and Continental writers who consider primitivism and civility, though he does not explore the implications for the idea of a renaissance. For travel literature, see Roy Harvey Pearce, "Primitivistic Ideas in the *Faerie Queene,*" *Journal of English and Germanic Philology* 44 (1945):139–51. For all the landscapes and ideals that underlie the whole discussion, see Arthur O. Lovejoy and George Boas, *Primitivism and Related Ideas in Antiquity* (Baltimore, 1935); George Boas, *Essays on Primitivism and Related Ideas in*

the Middle Ages (Baltimore, 1948); A. Bartlett Giamatti, *The Earthly Paradise and the Renaissance Epic* (Princeton, 1966); Harry Levin, *The Myth of the Golden Age in the Renaissance* (Bloomington, Ind., 1969); Joseph E. Duncan, *Milton's Earthly Paradise: A Historical Study of Eden* (Minneapolis, 1972). One should also see the massive work of Antonello Gerbi, *The Dispute of the New World: The History of a Polemic 1750–1950*, trans. Jeremy Moyle, rev. ed. (Pittsburgh, 1973) and, for bibliography and Hayden White's splendid essay, "The Forms of Wildness: Archaeology of an Idea," see the collection *The Wild Man Within: An Image in Western Thought from the Renaissance to Romanticism*, ed. Edward Dudley and Maximillian E. Novak (Pittsburgh, 1972). A brief overview of the contacts between the New World and the Old can be found in Sebastiano Lo Nigro, *Mondo primitivo ed Europa* (Catania, 1970). The Wild Man is touched on in Roderick Nash, *Wilderness and the American Mind*, rev. ed. (New Haven and London, 1973), pp. 12–13 and 47 f.; for wide ranging and useful bibliography touching most of these subjects and others, see his valuable "A Note on the Sources" and "Supplementary Note," pp. 274–88. Spenser is cited from the convenient *Complete Poetical Works of Spenser*, ed. R. E. N. Dodge (Boston, 1908).

4   Older editors printed *Americke* and some modern editors retain that spelling. See *Variorum*, ed. Ray Heffner, vol. 5 (Baltimore, 1936), critical note to V.x. 3.6 at p. 371; *The Faerie Queene*, ed. H. C. Hamilton (London and New York, 1977), using the text of J. C. Smith (Oxford, 1909), at p. 597; and *The Faerie Queene*, ed. T. P. Roche, Jr., with the assistance of C. P. O'Donnell, Jr. (New Haven and London, 1981), p. 1205. Heffner and Hamilton are certain Americke means America (as at *F. Q.* II.x.72). Roche offers the reader a choice of Brittany or America. I believe the context makes it clear that the New World is being referred to, and Dodge's adoption of Todd's conjectural *Americke* is most sensible.

5   By *foundling*, I intend any child lost, abandoned, or stolen, thus expanding on the OED: any "deserted infant whose parents are unknown, a child whom there is no one to claim," and including *changeling*, specifically as it occurs in *Midsummer-Night's Dream* II.i.23;120—the stolen child for whom another is substituted. For Wild Men, and bibliography about them, see the fine study of Penelope Doob, *Nebuchadnezzar's Children: Conventions of Madness in Middle English Literature* (New Haven and London, 1974), chapter 4, "The Unholy and the Holy Wild Man," especially pp. 135–37; for Wild Men in Spenser, see Donald Cheney, *Spenser's Image of Nature: Wild Man and Shepherd in "The Faerie Queene"* (New Haven, 1966) *passim*, of particular relevance here is chapter 5, "Wild Man and Shepherd," especially, pp. 196–214. Also see John Erskine Hankins, *Source and Meaning in Spenser's Allegory: A Study of The Faerie Queene* (Oxford, 1971), pp. 179–85. These views of Wild Men and their role in Spenser are very different from mine though not incompatible, save that I emphasize the limited potential of the Wild or Salvage Man. See also Robert H. Goldsmith, "The Wild Man on the English Stage," *Modern Language Review* 53 (1958):481–91; Herbert Foltinek, "Die Wilden Männer in Edmund Spensers 'Faerie Queene'," *Die Neueren Sprachen*, N.F. 10 (1961):493–512; A. S. Knowles, Jr., "Spenser's Natural Man," *Renaissance Papers 1958, 1959, 1960*, ed. G. W. Williams and P. G. Phialas, The Southeastern

Renaissance Conference 1961 (Durham, N.C., 1961), pp. 3–11, esp. 6. These references, and others, can be found in Humphrey Tonkin's good discussion, *Spenser's Courteous Pastoral: Book Six of the Faerie Queene* (Oxford, 1972), "Salvage Man," pp. 58–65, esp. 61–62.

6   I regret not having seen Barbara Estrin, "The Lost Child in Spenser's *The Faerie Queene*, Sidney's *Old Arcadia*, and Shakespeare's *The Winter's Tale*," (Ph.D. diss., Brown University, 1972), which, I gather from the abstract I have seen, has an outlook similar to mine on foundlings. See Nelson (n. 12 below).

7   See n. 5 above.

8   OED, s.v. *foundling*, cites Arthur Golding, *De Mornay*, Pref. 8 (1587): "As for lying or vntruth, it is a foundling, and not a thing bred"; s.v. *changeling*, George Puttenham, *The Arte of English Poesie* (1589): "Hipallage or the Changeling . . . as, he that should say, for tell me troth and lie not, lie me troth and tell not." Here Puttenham uses the figure and, in using it, refers to the shiftiness in language it figures. When the foundling (or changeling), either as infant or as language, is misused, it becomes monstrous (if a child) or makes us monstrous (if language). This is another way of saying that the possibility always remains that the foundling may reengage the primitive if care is not exercised.

9   In Book IV, there is Agape, the Fay, who, after being "oppressed" by a "noble youthly knight" in the "salvage wood" (IV.ii.45), had three sons, Priamond, Diamond, and Triamond," . . . in one happie mold, / Borne at one burden in one happie morne" (41). The episode recalls that of Chrysogone (III.vi.26–27) and the birth of Belphoebe and Amoret. Agape's sons grow up in a manner parallel to most of the foundlings in the poem.

10   His mother's influence is at issue: at one point she sees him with lion cubs and urges him: "leave off this dreadfull play; / . . . Go find some other play-fellowes, mine own sweet boy" (28).

11   I have touched on exile in epic in chapter 1 above, "The Forms of Epic." For a study of exile and the development of the Renaissance, see Margaret Williams Ferguson, "The Rhetoric of Exile in Du Bellay and His Classical Precursors" (Ph.D. diss., Yale University, 1974)—Ferguson's study of exile, and its insights into Renaissance theories of culture and language, is the most impressive examination of the subject I have seen.

12   Cheney, p. 208, and Hankins, p. 181, only mention the baby in passing; William Nelson, *The Poetry of Edmund Spenser* (New York, 1963), p. 288, does say: "The use of education is most clearly defined in the episode of the bear baby," and Nelson cites VI.iv.35 and notes that the child "may be molded into the form of a knight or learned man—or a learned poet." But the baby is then abandoned again. Kathleen Williams, *Spenser's World of Glass: A Reading of "The Faerie Queene"* (Berkeley and Los Angeles, 1966), p. 208, mentions the episode as an instance of "Fortune's long and witty foresight." Rosemary Freeman, *The Faerie Queene: A Companion for Readers* (Berkeley and Los Angeles, 1970), pp. 322–23, notes that the episode is part of the pastoral setting and based on Irish folklore—which is what the Variorum edition tells us (*The Works of Edmund Spenser*, ed. Edwin Greenlaw et al. [9 vols., Baltimore 1932–1949] Books VI and VII, pp. 204–05). The baby in Irish lore is

referred to in passing by Arnold Williams, *Flower on a Lowly Stalk; The Sixth Book of The Faerie Queene* (East Lansing, Mich., 1967), p. 71. Tonkin discusses Matilde and the baby "as a product of Spenser's own fancy, a texture of half-remembered associations and vaguely recollected reading" (p. 67); see the discussion, pp. 65–69, and, on the baby, pp. 219–25. Tonkin anticipates my comments on the baby as being formed for the active or contemplative life (p. 222, n. 29).

13 *Enchase*, from OF *enchâsser*, to enshrine, set (a gem), encase; from *en* and *châsse*, shrine, casket, case; from Lat. *capsa*. S.v. *enchase*, OED and *Oxford Dictionary of English Etymology*.

14 Gerioneo's knights will "enchace" Arthur's shield in an ironic parallel at V.x.34.

15 The rhyme of "enchaced" and "graced" is also used in *Amoretti* LXXXII. There the usage is wry and self-deprecatory: had only God graced her, as he had in other things, with a poet proper to enchase her.

Chapter 6: Marlowe

1 My text for Marlowe's plays is *The Complete Plays of Christopher Marlowe*, ed. Irving Rebner (New York, 1963). I am indebted to the notes of this fine edition.

2 Text from *Christopher Marlowe: The Complete Poems and Translations*, ed. Stephen Orgel (Harmondsworth and Baltimore, 1971).

Chapter 7: Proteus Unbound

Mr. Shane Gasbarra has provided invaluable scholarly assistance in the preparation of this volume for the Press, and particularly this chapter. I am grateful to him for his assistance in preparing translations and in checking texts.

1 Ed. Thomas Cooper (1559). Cooper, in his own *Thesaurus Linguae Romanae & Britannicae* (London, 1565), follows Elyot's account of Proteus verbatim. For the tradition of Proteus as king of Egypt, see the good study of Spenser by Thomas Roche, Jr., *The Kindly Flame* (Princeton, 1964), pp. 152–55. Unless otherwise noted, all references to Greek and Latin authors and all translations from Greek refer to the appropriate volume in the Loeb Classical Library.

2 Letter dated 19 July, no. 854 in *Opus Epistolarum Des. Erasmi Roterodami*, ed. P.S. Allen, H. M. Allen, and H.W. Garrod (Oxford, 1906–58) 3:353.

3 Letter dated 15 October, 3:402.

4 Vives, *Opera* (Basel, 1955), pp. 270–71. Text from the translation by Nancy Lenkeith in *The Renaissance Philosophy of Man*, ed. E. Cassirer, P.O. Kristeller, and J.H. Randall, Jr. (Chicago, 1948), pp. 389, 392.

5 I cite the *De Hominis Dignitate, Heptaplus, De Ente et Uno*, ed. E. Garin (Firenze, 1942), p. 106. The translations have been adapted from Elizabeth L. Forbes's translation in *The Renaissance Philosophy of Man*.

6 "Quis hunc nostrum chamaeleonta non admiretur?" (*De Hominis*, p. 106). The Chaldaean saying, p. 108. As Edgar Wind notes in his brilliant chapter "Pan and Proteus" in *Pagan Mysteries in the Renaissance* (New Haven, 1958), p. 158, Ficino

uses the same argument. The chameleon was commonly associated with Proteus; cf. Erasmus, *Epitome Adagiorum* (Amsterdam, 1650), s.v. "Chameleonte Mutabilior" and "Proteo Mutabilior." Subsequent references to the *Adages* (1500) will be to the third or Aldine edition (Venice, 1508) or *Desiderii Erasmus Operum Omnium* (Leiden, 1703–06).

7   *De Hominis,* p. 108.

8   Ibid., pp. 138–40.

9   Wind, *Pagan Mysteries,* p. 158, cites Pico in "one of the Orphic *Conclusiones*: 'He who cannot attract Pan, approaches Proteus in vain'"; he continues: "The advice to seek for the hidden Pan in the ever-changing Proteus refers to the principle of 'the whole in the part,' of the One inherent in the Many." Associated with this quest for truth under disguises was the Silenus Alcibiades which derives from Plato's *Symposium,* 215, where Alcibiades compares Socrates to the statuettes of Silenus. See Erasmus' *Adagia,* s.v. "Silenus Alcibiades," *Opera Omnia,* 2.7700–82c, esp. 770d, and Wind, *Pagan Mysteries,* p. 179. In the *Enchiridion* (trans. R. Himelick [Bloomington, 1965]), Erasmus says: "the Holy Scriptures, like the Silenus of Alcibiades, conceal their real divinity beneath a surface that is crude and almost laughable" (p. 105). Jacob Cats called a book of emblems *Silenus Alcibiades sive Proteus* (1618); cf. on this and the role of emblem books, Wind, p. 137.

10 *De Hominis,* p. 162.

11 My text is the *Essais,* ed. M. Rat, Classiques Garnier, 2 vols. (Paris, 1962) 2:222. The translations here and below have been adapted from *The Complete Essays of Montaigne,* trans. Donald M. Frame (Stanford, 1958). This quotation is from "Du Repentir."

12 "De Trois Commerces," *Essais,* 2:238, 237.

13 "Du Repentir," ibid., pp. 237, 222.

14 "De La Vanité," ibid., p. 431.

15 "Par Divers Moyen On Arrive A Pareille Fin," ibid., 1:5.

16 "De La Vanité," ibid., 2:431; for Solon below, see p. 433.

17 Ibid., p. 446.

18 *The Anatomy of Melancholy,* ed. A. R. Shilleto, intro. A. H. Bullen (London, Bohn's Standard Library, 1920) 1:443.

19 Cf. Silius Italicus, *Punica,* VII.436; Valerius Flaccus, *Argonautica,* II.318; Ovid, *Metamorphoses,* II.9. In Orphic theology, all the gods are "dei ambigui," that is, as Wind (*Pagan Mysteries,* p. 161) says, they are "animated by a law of self-contrariety" and, later (p. 162), they are seen "both as inciters and as moderators." A better description of Proteus and of his roles could not be found.

20 *Faust,* II.iii.8152–487; cf. Shelley's "The Proteus Shape of Nature as It Slept," *Triumph of Life,* 271. For Proteus as a natural philosopher, see below, p. 124. For Browne, see *The Gardens of Cyrus,* in *Works,* ed. G. Keynes, new ed. (Chicago, 1964) 1:225. I am indebted to Michael O'Loughlin for this reference. Francis Bacon, in *The Wisdom of the Ancients* (XIII), states that "the person of Proteus denotes matter, the oldest of all things, after God Himself" (*The Moral and Historical Works* . . . , ed. J. Devey [London, Bohn's Standard Library, 1854], p. 227); see also Andrea Alciati s.v. emblem clxxxii in *Omnia Andrea Alciati V.C. Emblemata*

(Antwerp, 1581), p. 633. Bacon's source was obviously the great work of Natalis Comes (Natale Conti), *Mythologiae sive Explicationis Fabularum* (1551), VIII.8. See the edition I cite throughout, Hanoviae (1619), pp. 850−51. See also the very influential work of Carolo Stephanus (Charles Estienne), *Dictionarium Historicum, Geographicum, Poeticum* (Geneva, 1652), col. 1677. First published in 1553, I cite the Geneva edition throughout.

21   For Theodulph, see "De Libris quos legere solebam," in the *Patrologia Latina*, ed. J.P. Migne, 105.331−32. Theodulph's statement is part of the long Christian tradition of seeing truth under the veil of fiction. Cf. Boccaccio, *Genealogie Deorum Gentilium Libri*, XIV.7, in the translation of Books XIV and XV by C. G. Osgood, *Boccaccio on Poetry* (Princeton, 1930), p. 157, n. 8, where the concept is traced from Augustine to Milton; cf. Erasmus on Silenus Alcibiades and Holy Scripture, above, n. 9. On Proteus and how to "temperare la fizzione poetica et ornare le cose sacre con le profane . . . " in his *De Partu Virginis*, see Jacopo Sannazaro's letter of 13 April 1521 in *Opere Volgari*, ed. A. Mauro (Bari, 1961), p. 373. Near the beginning of his *Davideis*, Abraham Cowley promises "T'unbind the charms that in slight *Fables* lie, / And teach that *Truth* is truest *Poesie*" (ll.41−42 in *Poems*, ed. A. R. Waller [Cambridge, 1905], p. 243)—the image is a Christian reversal of Proteus, now unbinding, not fettering, to grasp the truth. For Chaucer, see *Romaunt*, 6319−22 in *Works*, ed. F. R. Robinson, 2d ed. (Cambridge, Mass., 1957), p. 624.

22   The epithet "blue" later occurs in Silius Italicus, *Punica*, VII.420, at the beginning of Proteus' long prophecy on the fate of Italy; cf. "blue Proteus" in Ben Jonson, *Volpone*, III.vii.153 (discussed below), and Shelley, *Prometheus Bound*, III.ii.24.

23   See also Lucan, *Pharsalia*, X.511 ff. Thetis, who prophesied to Achilles, *Iliad*, XVIII.34−147, is also a sea creature allied with Proteus' vatic powers. Cf. Plato, *Republic*, 2.381d. In Ovid, *Metamorphoses*, XI.224, Proteus foresees a great son for Thetis; she then (249−65) changes shapes to escape Proteus.

24   For Boccaccio, VII.9, I use the Scrittori d'Italia edition of the *Genealogie Deorum Gentilium*, ed. V. Romano (Bari, 1951) I: 343; Erasmus, *Adagia* (1508), pp. 130−31, and in *Opera Omnia*, 2. 473b−74a; see the epigraph to this essay from the third edition of Elyot's *Bibliotheca*, ed. Cooper; Alciati, *Emblemata*, pp. 629−30; Comes, *Mythologiae*, p. 854; Vincenzo Cartari, *Le Imagini, con la Spositione de i Dei degli Antichi* (1556), for which I use the revised and corrected edition (Lyon, 1581), p. 214; Bacon, *Wisdom of the Ancients* (XIII), p. 227; Alexander Ross, *Mystagogus Poeticus or The Muses Interpreter* (London, 1647), p. 191.

25   See Osgood, *Boccaccio*, pp. xxxviii and 46, n. 23, for source in Isidore and ancients; p. xlii for idea in Alberto Mussato.

26   Text in *Elizabethan Critical Essays*, ed. G. G. Smith (Oxford, 1904), I:154, 159.

27   Ibid., p. 156.

28   For instance, wisdom was commonly attributed to Proteus; see Ross, *Mystagogus Poeticus*, p. 191, after Comes, *Mythologiae*, p. 854.

29   *Poems*, 9th ed. (London, 1712), p. 99; I am indebted again to Michael O'Loughlin for this reference. Champfleury (Jules Husson, dit Fleury, 1821−89), cited by René Wellek, *A History of Modern Criticism* (New Haven and London, 1965)

4: 473, in n. 14 to p. 2. In "The Poet" Emerson describes the poet as "the man without impediment, who sees and handles what others dream of, traverses the whole scale of experience" (*Essays: Second Series* [New York, John W. Lovell Co., n.d.], p. 8). Emerson's language suggests a Proteus and sounds like Keats's notion of "*Negative Capability,* that is when man is capable of being in uncertainties, Mysteries, doubts, without any irritable reaching after fact & reason." Here too the language for the poet is reminiscent of Proteus. See letter of 27 December 1817 to George and Tom Keats, in *The Letters of John Keats,* ed. H. E. Rollins (Cambridge, Mass., 1958) I:193.

30   It is interesting that Silius Italicus, *Punica,* VII, says Proteus knows "arcana deum" (424) and so the prophet will begin far back in order to reveal the future (436–37); this knowledge of the gods and this method of telling are very similar to what Silius says of himself at the opening of the epic (I.17–20).

   Bacon, *Wisdom of the Ancients* (XIII), also calls Proteus "the revealer and inter-preter of all antiquity, and secrets of every kind." This admirably describes Bacon's own role; see his *Preface,* especially the end (pp. 227, 203).

31   Comes, *Mythologiae,* p. 852. Milton's *Elegia Tertia,* 26, and *Epitaphium Damonis,* 99, refer conventionally to Proteus as herdsman under the sea, while Marlowe (*Dido, Queen of Carthage,* I.i.76–77) has followed Horace (*Odes,* I.ii.7) in a bizarre vision of water flooding the land and Proteus driving his herd in treetops. Horace never has much good to say for Proteus: cf. *Epistles,* I.i.90, and *Satires,* II.iii.71. Spenser is attracted by neither Proteus (called "unlovely," *Faerie Queene,* IV.xi.2) nor his charges: "his heard / Of stinking seales and porcpisces" (*Colin Clouts Come Home Againe,* 248–49). I cite Spenser from *The Complete Poetical Works . . . ,* ed. R.E.N. Dodge (Boston, 1936).

32   Sannazaro's pioneering claim ignores, as W.P. Mustard has indicated, "certain of the Idyls of Theocritus (VI, XI, XXI), an author whom Sannazaro knew very well." See Mustard's edition, *The Piscatory Eclogues of Jacopo Sannazaro* (Baltimore, 1914), p. 14.

33   *Eclogues,* ed. Mustard, p. 78; cf: Tasso's Proteus as "sacro marin pastore," in *Intermedio* I to the *Aminta* in *Opere,* ed. Bruno Maier (Milano, 1963) I:206.

34   See *Eclogues,* ed. Mustard, p. 84f. Sannazaro's line on Proteus' song: "laetus cantabat ad auras" (29) echoes Virgil, *Eclogue* I.56: "canet frondatur ad auras," as well as Virgil, *Eclogue* VI.31ff.: "Namque canebat" (see Mustard, p. 85). At line 23, Sannazaro's "divino carmine" echoes his own comment on Proteus in his *Eclogue* I.88 and Virgil's on Linus in *Eclogue* VI.67, both cited above in the text.

35   I.xi in *Opere Volgari,* ed. Mauro, p. 143.

36   Comes, *Mythologiae,* p. 854.

37   *De Hominis,* pp. 148–54.

38   Tasso, *Rime,* "Come sia Proteo o mago," in *Opere,* ed. Maier, I:391; cf. also p. 500. Milton refers to the "*Carpathian* wizard's hook" in *Comus,* 872. Comes, p. 854. Boccaccio, *Genealogie,* XIV.6; XIV.7 (see Osgood, *Boccaccio,* pp. 39, 40, and passim; notions of craft are also at issue: p. 158, n. 16), refers constantly to poetry as an art, and he also devotes a section (XIV.16; Osgood, pp. 76–78) to combating the pejorative designation of the poet as "seductor" or enchanter of men's minds.

Osgood, p. 176, n. 6, shows how Boccaccio used the same word which was applied to Christ, Matt. 27:63. The (ancient, Platonic) objection Boccaccio was fighting, however, is related to the potential for evil in the poet's power which we have been discussing, and the idea achieved currency simply in Boccaccio's widely read condemnation of it.

39 *Opere Volgari,* ed. Mauro, pp. 43–44.

40 *Euthydemus,* 288c. Earlier Socrates described the pair as possessing such "skill in the war of words, that they can refute any proposition whether true or false" (272b). I cite Plato throughout from the four-volume *The Dialogues of Plato,* trans. B. Jowett, 4th ed. rev. (Oxford, 1953).

41 Abraham Fraunce, in *The third part of the Countess of Pembrokes Iuychurch* (London, 1592), says: "Plato *compareth him to the wrangling of brabling sophisters: and some there be that hereby understand, the truth of things obscured by so many deceauable appearences*" (cited in Roche, *Kindly Flame,* p. 159). Alciati, *Emblemata,* "Plerique vatem faciunt, alii Oratorem, vel Sophistam" (p. 634); and Stephanus, *Dictionarium,* "Plato in Euthydemo exponit de fallaciis quibus sophistae in disputando utuntur" (col. 1677). Without reference to Plato, Sir Thomas More compares a sophistic theologian to Proteus in his long letter to Martin Dorp defending Erasmus. See his letter of 21 October 1515, in *St. Thomas More: Selected Letters,* ed. E. F. Rogers, Yale Edition, Modernized Series (New Haven and London, 1961), p. 31.

42 Text from Loeb Classical Library's *Petronius* (and Seneca, *Apocolocyntosis*), p. 302. Compare Oenothea's ability to disturb nature with Proteus in Horace, *Odes,* I.ii.7.

43 Circe represented the most dangerous impulses to self-destruction in the human soul while she masqueraded as the fulfillment of every man's deepest desires. For Circe, see A. B. Giamatti, *The Earthly Paradise and the Renaissance Epic* (Princeton, 1966), passim, and, for a different emphasis on her as an agent of illusion, the excellent unpublished dissertation of Richard Saéz, "The Redemptive Circe: Illusion and The Beneficence of Evil in Tasso, Milton and Calderón" (Ph.D. diss., Yale University, 1967).

44 Text from *Torquato Tasso Poesie e Prose,* ed. S. A. Nulli (Milano, 1955).

45 *Proteus Redivivus,* pp. 3, 5. The title page tells us the book was "Collected and Methodized by the Author of the First Part of the English Rogue." This would be Richard Head (1637?–1686?), whose *English Rogue, described in the Life of Meriton Latroon. Being a Compleat History of the Most Eminent Cheats,* appeared in 1665. For Head's other writings, some in collaboration with Francis Kirkman, see *The Cambridge Bibliography of English Literature,* 2:176–77, 529–30, 930. Head's labors were not only Protean but Herculean.

46 "Conversation," meaning familiar discourse (16th c.) as well as intercourse, acquaintance, or mode of living (17th c.), from OF *conversacion, −tion,* from L. *conversatiō (n)* (conduct, frequent use or abode), from *conversārī,* a middle use of *conversāre,* to turn around, from *con + versāre,* a frequent form of (*con*) *vertere,* to turn or to transform. "Convert," from OF *convertir,* from L. *convertere.* See the *OED* and *The Oxford Dictionary of English Etymology,* ed. C. T. Onions and others (Oxford, 1966), s.v. "convert," "conversation," and, for the latter, "converse." It is also interesting to note that the epithet "ambiguus," traditionally used by classical

poets for Proteus (see above, n. 19) maintains the sense of turning, being formed on *ambi* (around) and *ago, -ere* (to go).

47 My text is *The Complete Plays of Christopher Marlowe*, ed. Irving Ribner (New York, 1963).

48 Text in *The Dunciad*, ed. James Sutherland (Twickenham ed. London, 1943) 5:272–73. It is interesting to note that these lines were added to the final edition of 1743 (Sutherland's B text, which I cite). Compare the version of 1728 (A) in Sutherland, p. 64. For Warburton's note, cited in part below, see p. 272.

49 For other monsters, see I.81, 106. After writing this, I found my sense of Proteus' function confirmed and enlarged in the study of A. Kernan, "*The Dunciad* and the Plot of Satire," reprinted in *Essential Articles for the Study of Alexander Pope*, ed. M. Mack (Hamden, Conn., 1964), pp. 726–38, where the shapeless, disordering powers of Dulness are discussed.

50 *The Dunciad*, ed. Sutherland, p. 393. Cibber and others had been referred to as wizards at III.265ff. It is generally agreed that the Wizard figures Walpole.

51 Text in Loeb Classical Library's *Lucian*, trans. Harmon, 5:231–32. See Erasmus, *Adagia*, p. 130, and *Opera Omnia*, 2:473b; Comes, *Mythologiae*, p. 852; Alciati, *Emblemata*, p. 634; Stephanus, *Dictionarium*, col. 1677. Sir John Davies, in his splendid "Orchestra, or a poem of Dancing," 561–67, has also remembered his Lucian. For Tasso, see *Opere*, ed. Maier, I:205–06, and editor's note.

52 Jean Rousset, in his *La Littérature de l'age Baroque en France* (Paris, 1953), links Circe, as we have, with Proteus—"il est sa propre Circé, comme Circé fait du monde un immense Protée. Le magicien de soi-même et la magicienne d'autrui étaient destinés à s'associer pour donner figure à l'un des mythes de l'époque: l'homme multiforme dans un monde en métamorphose" (p. 22). Stephen Orgel, in *The Jonsonian Masque* (Cambridge, Mass., 1965), opens by discussing *The Mask of Proteus and The Adamantine Rock*, presented at Gray's Inn, Shrovetide, 1595 (see edition by W. W. Greg, *Gesta Grayorum, 1688* [Oxford, Malone Society Reprints, 1914]). Like Rousset, Orgel believes that Proteus was "the mythological representative of two central themes of the literature of the age: the dangers of inconstancy and the deceptiveness of appearances" (p.10).

53 My text throughout is *The Complete Works of Shakespeare*, ed. G. L. Kittredge (Boston, Ginn and Co., 1936).

54 Text, with *v* normalized to *u*, from *Works*, ed. C. H. Herford and P. and E. Simpson (Oxford, 1925–52), 5; commentary in 9.

55 See Kernan's introduction, to which I am indebted, to his edition of *Volpone*, The Yale Ben Jonson (New Haven, 1962), pp. 11ff. Kernan specifically adduces Pico, pp. 14–15.

56 Herford and Simpson, eds., *Works*, 9:720, cite Martial, X.v.17; for Lucian, see Loeb edition, 3:161.

57 Text in *Minor Elizabethan Epics*, ed. E. S. Donno (New York and London, 1963), p. 53; see through l. 156. Marlowe is looking back at the carvings on the palace of the sun, where Proteus is mentioned, in Ovid, *Metamorphoses*, II.9.

58 Boccaccio, *Genealogie*, VII.9: "Formas vero, quas eum sumere consuetum aiunt, et abicere, eas existimo passiones, quibus aguntur homines" (ed. Romano, I:344); Alciati, *Emblemata*, p. 633; Erasmus, *Opera Omnia*, 5:18c–d.

59   Cartari, *Imagini*, p. 225; Erasmus, *Adagia*, p. 130; Milton, *Paradise Lost*, IX.393–
      95, used the deceitful and sensual implications of this story in treating Eve and her
      seduction by Satan (see Giamatti, *Earthly Paradise*, pp. 327ff.). The name Ver-
      tumnus is derived from *verto, -ere*, to turn or to transform, the same root discussed in
      relation to Proteus. See above, n. 46.

60   The hermit is called a magician in VIII.67 and X.94. This fact, his age, and the
      marine locale serve to parody Proteus as they anticipate him. Text from *Orlando
      Furioso*, ed. Nicola Zingarelli, 6th ed. (Milano, 1959). The translations that follow
      have been adapted from *Orlando Furioso, An English Prose Translation*, by Guido
      Waldman (Oxford University Press, 1974).

61   Spenser, *Faerie Queene*, III.viii.29ff., tells the story of Proteus' rescue and attempted
      rape of Florimell. There is some humor in Proteus' assault and Ariosto (*Orlando
      Furioso*, VIII.29ff.) is obviously being used, but the "civil" concerns of the Italian
      are not part of Spenser's purpose. For a full discussion of sources, see the Variorum
      edition, ed. E. Greenlaw and others (Baltimore, 1932–49; index, 1957) 3:
      269–72; for good critical commentary, see Roche, *Kindly Flame*, pp. 158–62.

62   *Renaissance Philosophy*, p. 389.

63   Comes, *Mythologiae*, pp. 854–55. See also Ross, *Mystagogus Poeticus*, pp. 191ff.

64   See *Narrative and Dramatic Sources of Shakespeare*, ed. G. Bullough (London and New
      York, 1957) I:203–11 (intro.), 212–66 (texts of sources).

65   Arther Quiller-Couch and J. Dover Wilson in their Cambridge edition of the play
      (Cambridge, 1921) were forcibly struck, but not dumb; for their detection of other
      hands, see their introduction, pp. xiii–xix, and notes to V.iv, pp. 102–04.

Index